THE ULTIMATE SUCCESS SYSTEM FOR LIFE

"BECAUSE REAL SUCCESS IS ABOUT WHO YOU BECOME ALONG THE WAY"

Copyright © 2024 by Steven Mackie

All rights reserved. No part of this publication may be reproduced, distributed, or transmitted in any form or by any means, including photocopying, recording, or other electronic or mechanical methods, without the prior written permission of the publisher, except in the case of brief quotations embodied in critical reviews and certain other noncommercial uses permitted by copyright law.

A Note From the Author

I'm not a doctor, therapist, or expert. I'm a 56-year-old man from the north east of England who has lived what seems like 20 lives, stumbled, and fell a million times, risen more times than a ghost who refuses to take the hint, learned life's lessons the hard way even when the lesson was easy, and searched for answers when I wasn't even sure what the question was.

This book is simply a collection of my own thoughts, experiences, and research.

What you'll find here is a system (the ultimate success system) not a set of rules or a gospel truth. It is a working guide of ideas and practices that have helped me and may help you. Some things will hopefully resonate, some may not, and that's okay. Take what serves you, leave what doesn't, if it helps then feel free to share it.

If you need medical, financial, or professional advice, please seek it from qualified experts. My hope is only that these pages spark a transformational journey of positive change in your life, by offering reflection, encouragement, and practical steps by following a system that offers a path toward living a more fulfilling and purposeful life.

In the end, this is the ultimate success system for life that I used to transform my life. My wish is that it inspires you to enjoy the process and build your own.

Steven Mackie

Question
What is a system and how do you make a successful one.

Answer
A system is a set of interconnected components or elements that work together to achieve a common goal.

To create a successful system we need to define clear objectives, ensure effective communication between components, anticipate potential issues, and regularly evaluate and adapt the system based on feedback and changing requirements.
A successful system for human life involves maintaining a balance across various aspects or habits. We shall call these habits The Magnificent Seven and once you understand how these habits interconnect and support one another then you can take control of your life in ways you only dreamed of.
With discipline, integrity and consistency, regular self-reflection and adaptation, these seven habits form the foundational pillars or the blueprint for the ultimate success system for your life.

Remember, these habits can take a lifetime to master, so be patient with yourself as each habit will clearly let you know where you are in life and give you the understanding of why.
Today is the day you begin to transform into who you will be for the rest of your life.

"The only person you are destined to become is the person you decide to be." - Ralph Waldo Emerson

So make a conscious decision now of who you want to be and begin the journey of reimagining yourself. Begin to form an idea in your mind of exactly what you and your life looks like then ask yourself, "who must I become in order for this to be my life, the life I choose to live every day".

What Are The Top Ten Things you Currently Value Most in Your Life

1..

2..

3..

4..

5..

6..

7..

8..

9..

10..

We will come back to this later.

This Book is Dedicated to the Curious of Mind

This book is for those who question, explore, and seek meaning beyond the surface, and has been designed as a manifesto of wonder to inspire and capture the imagination of those who seek the often hidden simple joys that life has to offer if one is paying attention.

There is something inherently magical about curiosity. It is the fire at the beginning of every discovery, the pulse that moves the human spirit toward the unknown. Within these pages lies a journey not meant to be walked by everyone, but by those who are willing to ask, to wonder, to imagine.

Curiosity is often dismissed as childlike or naive, but that is a misunderstanding of its power. Curiosity is not ignorance; it is the rejection of stagnation. It is the acknowledgment that the world, and the self is unfinished, layered, complex. It is the refusal to accept things at face value. In a world that too often rewards certainty, conformity, and comfort, curiosity is an act of quiet rebellion.

Although the book begins with a short story, this isn't about me it's about you, and what you are willing to explore.
This is an invitation to slow down and pay attention. In the age of noise, speed, and instant gratification, curiosity asks you to linger and reread a sentence because something about it tugged at your mind.

If you've ever wondered what's beneath the surface of life, of stories, of yourself, then this is for you.

We live in a time when skepticism often replaces wonder, and knowing everything is more prized than seeking something. To be curious today is to reclaim a kind of sacred attention. What is being offered is an open door, with the quiet confidence that the right people will walk through it, and in doing so turn on a light.

And just like that…………your journey begins.

Let me begin your journey with a lie, the biggest lie you were ever told.

It's Not That Simple

The biggest lie you were ever told is a script from the movie Bleed for This, where boxer Vinny Pazienza (Miles Tellers character) tells a journalist that the biggest lie he was told was, "It's not that simple". He explains this is a phrase used to discourage people.

Here's the full exchange from the film's scene:

Female Reporter: "So what would you say the biggest deception was? What was the biggest lie you were told?"

Vinny Pazienza: "It's not that simple."

Female Reporter: "Why not?"

Vinny Pazienza: "No, that's the biggest lie I was ever told. It's not that simple, and it's a lie they tell you over and over again."

Female Reporter: "What's not simple?"

Vinny Pazienza: "Any of it. All of it. It's how they get you to give up. They say, It's not that simple, Vinny."

Female Reporter: "So, what's the truth?"

Vinny Pazienza: "That it is, and if you just do the thing they tell you you can't then it's done, and you realise it is that simple, and that it always was."

Contents

Introduction.	My Story
Chapter 1.	The Magnificent Seven
Chapter 2.	Primary Habits, Secondary Habits and Occasional Activities
Chapter 3.	Distractions
Chapter 4.	Making the Change
Chapter 5.	Time
Chapter 6.	Today's Challenges
Chapter 7.	Emotional Elasticity
Chapter 8.	It's All Connected
Chapter 9.	Perception vs Perspective
Chapter 10.	Pyramid of Success
Chapter 11.	Deeper Thoughts
Chapter 12.	The Path Forward
Chapter 13.	Philosophical Insights
Chapter 14.	Life is a Skill

Acknowledgements.

Introduction - My Story

As a 52 year old overweight man from the North East of England life was pretty good or so I thought, business was going well, and things were moving in a positive direction, when suddenly the pandemic hit in early 2020 triggering a global upheaval, initiating lockdowns, travel restrictions, and economic slowdowns worldwide.

As nations grappled with overwhelmed healthcare systems, shortages of medical supplies, and a surge in COVID-19 cases, suddenly we entered the twilight zone and the world began to morph into this unrecognisable whole other thing.

The global economy suffered a severe downturn, causing widespread unemployment and financial strain.
Vaccine development and distribution efforts became focal points for recovery and I find myself sitting watching it all unfold on TV imagining I was caught up in some dystopian movie.

Simultaneously, socio-political tensions escalated. The Black Lives Matter movement gained momentum globally, highlighting systemic racism and advocating for social justice, and for some reason people were running round buying lots of toilet rolls.

People were kicking off all over the place protesting and statues of controversial historical figures were being torn down by groups who appeared to have clearly ran out of said toilet paper and needed to let off something hot and steamy of their own somehow.

Climate change concerns persisted, evidenced by extreme weather events and increased awareness about sustainability, and little Greta Thunberg was having a field day telling every man and his dog we were all doomed and it was all the fault of grown ups. Meanwhile I'm sitting scratching my backside thinking it would be over in a week or so before the next disaster exploded onto our screens to keep the fear locked in.

The UK faced its share of challenges The government implemented various lockdowns to attempt to curb virus spread, impacting businesses and daily life, and for some reason people could only purchase 2 tins of beans not 3 (unless you went to another shop and just bought more of this now deemed, high value item).

Brexit, finalised in January 2020, which led to negotiations over trade agreements and adjustments to new regulations. Vaccine rollout campaigns brought hope to many, but concerns about variants and public health policies persisted, meanwhile I'm preparing for the zombie apocalypse by stockpiling essentials (well buying a few extra tins of beans and some extra rice as well as enough wine to make a small French village blush).

Domestically, the UK witnessed shifts in leadership. Boris Johnson's government faced criticism over the handling of the pandemic, however Matt Hancock, Mr touchy feely social distance pleasy seemed to be doing alright for himself, shortening his social distance like a pro, as he was caught on camera touching up some female, after standing on telly telling kids not to kill their grannies, what a hero.
Criticisms came thick and fast especially regarding lockdown timings and policy clarity. Socially, debates on racial inequality, mental health support, and education reform intensified. Economically, the country grappled with job losses, business closures, and the intricacies of navigating post-Brexit trade relationships. Additionally, the 'pingdemic' (people being notified by NHS COVID-19 app to isolate) affected various sectors, leading to staff shortages and disruptions.

Basically all common sense had evaporated and chaos had ensued with television reports of grown up people now fighting over said previously mentioned toilet roll as if rushing to the toilet had become the number one post news update activity as I shout at the t.v "that'll be all the beans".

On a personal level my income had dropped to zero as businesses closed and tenants in my multi occupancy housing disappeared to move in with family when social distancing rules came in, leaving me with some tough decisions to make.

At the same time I begin to notice my clothes were getting tight due to my local gym being closed and my consumption of wine and poor eating decisions had increased and was becoming a regular habit.

My sedentary new lifestyle of total isolation and my new found "past caring" attitude to life was beginning to affect my mental health and I found myself constantly shouting at the television at every opportunity, mostly aimed at the educated elites in charge, who appeared to be making it up as they went along and were clueless as to what to do next other than parroting something about following the science in order to flatten the curve, meanwhile my curves were increasing and my back end was starting to feel like a doughnut in a deep fat fryer.

As the world navigated successive pandemic waves, vaccination efforts accelerated, enabling the gradual easing of restrictions, and a little fabric mask continued to be hailed as the saviour of humanity as well as becoming the new cigarette packet people were discarding with great regularity upon the street, despite the ever increasing boast of a climate emergency and our need to save the planet (never any mention of saving humanity from all this insanity).

The emergence of new COVID-19 variants added uncertainty, prompting ongoing debates about the balance between reopening and public safety as the politicians continued to step out on tv and tell the nation that everybody needed to follow the rules.

Amid these challenges, society witnessed remarkable resilience and adaptability, well when I say resilience I mean the police started locking grannies up for getting a bit fresh air and stopping for 5 minutes to sit on a park bench even though there was nobody else around, talk about protecting and serving, " this is what happens when you give little people some authority" I shout out, despite the fact that yet again there was nobody there to hear me.

Remote work became prevalent, accelerating digital transformation. Communities displayed solidarity through mutual aid initiatives, and people were clapping and banging on pans at their front doors in support of the NHS emphasising the importance of collective support during the crises. I personally refrained from engaging in this activity as banging pans outside my front door just isn't my thing, and in a different time would have had the men in white coats turning up to offer me a long sleeved shirt and a lift.

The post-lockdown period signified a landscape of rebuilding, redefining global relationships, and reimagining approaches to health, economy, and societal challenges, fostering a path toward recovery and adaptation in an ever-evolving world.
By this time I'm waiting for the aliens to land and save the day, in order to add another dimension to the increasing drama that appeared to get worse by the day as I poured myself another pinot noir and necked a microwaved pasty, the classy bloke that I am.

Then the news broke that Johnson and Hancock (there's a joke in there somewhere) as well as some of the other members in charge had not been following their own rules so it all kicked off and I find myself shouting at the telly again like a lunatic, "bunch of hypocrites!"
This led to more drinking and more bad eating decisions on my part as the F**ks I had once given were disappearing as rapidly as a rabbit down a hole.

Suddenly a new saviour stepped forth by the name of Liz Truss a once Liberal Democrat who, having watched her speak appeared to me to have the IQ of a ginger biscuit and the charisma of a pork scratching, was now in charge so things were bound to instantly change for the better.....Not!

The world I once knew had changed forever as people returned to work, but not really as they were now frightened of their own shadows and many worked from home where Zoom calls had become a major thing. This led to regular hilarity and an increase in YouTube videos as a lot of people were totally clueless (and often naked), and cats became YouTube famous.

A new trend had taken hold of the youth and something called gender pro nouns were now all the rage as people began identifying as whatever they wanted, boys were girls and girls were boys and some were even cats and foxes. Even the tv media were having trouble with it all.

Piers Morgan was identifying as a 2 spirit penguin and was being berated by some obnoxious smug mummy's boy with the boo hoo's named Benjamin Butterworth who was wanting Piers to be cancelled and sacked, or castrated or something, I don't know, nobody really gave a monkeys hoopla..

I on the other hand was happily identifying as a fat drunken jabba who was way beyond caring and wished I could jump in my delorean and go back to 1985, when the music was great, movies were great, people were great, social media and mobile phones didn't exist and life appeared at that time, at least for me, to hold great promise.

By this time none of my clothes fit me as I'm now like a house end and as a result of the lockdown and my income having virtually disappeared, I now find myself working as a driver bearer at a local funeral directors, for the lols.

I start going back to the gym but it was a total nightmare, as I couldn't run more than 10 steps without blowing out my giant back end and I'm still in the habit of drinking wine and eating garbage on an evening out of habit and boredom and a sense of "well I'm 52 and with everything that's going on why care?"

Then a few things happen that began to stir me from my cloudy existence.

On a night out for a friends birthday one of the lads I went to school with pulled me to one side and said "you were always the fit one, what happened?"

I remember getting angry and snapping "I've just joined the over 50's fat club and it's much easier, as you would know you cunky chunt".
At least my North East humour had not deserted me.

I began to notice however that I had developed some anger issues as a result of my long period of isolation.

Funny thing was I was still going to the gym but it was having zero effect due to the alcohol and food intake. To add to this I wasn't sleeping as I was up all night stumbling to the loo, and the full stomach was keeping me awake.

Then suddenly I found myself habitat fluid and fiscally challenged…….no I didn't, I was on the verge of being homeless and I was proper skint.

The house I'd been living in since the lockdown was my rental property, as when the world stopped I lost my income and as a result, could no longer afford the house I was renting which I'd lived in for 5 years, so had to move in to my HZO (House of Zero Occupation) when all my tenants disappeared as the social distancing rules came in.

Following the relaxing of the rules I managed to rent my house out as a single let and cadge a spare bed at a mates who was single, but if I'm honest I'd lost the will to live by this time and was surviving day to day basically wishing I'd go to sleep and not wake up as i felt the world had turned to garbage.

The country was in the toilet and Trusty Liz appeared to have made it worse in the 40 odd days she'd been in charge, and I remember shouting at the telly "I told you so, what do you expect when you put someone in charge with the mental capacity of a cheese toastie, pork markets my arse, this lunatic thinks she's running a lemonade stand!"

My sense of perspective was clearly failing as my alcohol consumption increased even further as my hope for a better future was being flushed right down the pan.

Then I wake one morning with the disease and I think, this is it my numbers up as I test positive. In that moment I had to laugh as I realised the only thing in my life that was positive was a bloody covid test.

I prepare myself for the worst and lock myself away, retiring to the bedroom with a bottle of glayva whiskey liqueur and some crisps thinking "If this is it I'm going out like a trooper, pour the whiskey and bring on the dancing girls and lets party, before the lights go out."

I sweat like mad for 14 days, all the fillings fall out of my teeth and everything tastes like metal, I'm dizzy as a duck every time I stand up, and I'm wiped out just going to the loo and feel like I have the energy levels of the splattered moth that was smudged on the toilet window sill.

After a few weeks of this I wake up one day and I'm fine, I've survived and I'm like "ah bollocks! I'm still here."
I turn the telly to the news the Queen had passed bless her, and now we've got some slimy little posh boy as Prime Minister who's worth a reported 400 million but decides he wants a hundred grand a year job "There's a rabbit away somewhere," I shout out in my Covid free and now totally paranoid capacity.

I also see that now instead of people standing at their doors clapping for the NHS, these same showers of excrement in charge are now demonising the NHS staff and sacking them for not taking the jab. The country is divided on yet another issue with the unvaxed being labelled stupid and selfish, and yet again I'm ranting, "aye I bet if they came on telly saying the science said in order to save more lives we all need to get our right arms chopped off, there'd be a queue round the block."

Meanwhile none of this is helping me and my situation and I'm now officially the fattest fatty ever touching 19 stones and I'm getting no sleep, drinking alcohol like water and eating garbage just about every day.

'm in a job that barely pays the rent and I'm more skint than I've ever been, and I'm just totally hating on the alive people for reasons best known to nobody as the only decent conversations I'm having are with the poor people who are deceased, despite it being a one way conversation.

My attitude was clearly requiring some adjustment and I needed to address the whole, "my worlds shit, my life's shit, I look like shit, I feel like shit, I don't care anymore and I can't be arsed, screw it all, pass me another drink," attitude.

Then one day I caught myself looking in the mirror.

The mirror never lies and the more I stared the more I felt my reflection was staring back at me and looking deep into my soul, asking me the question, "is that all?"

I felt like Iorek Byrnison the drunken polar bear from the movie The Golden Compass.
My armour had been stolen and I felt without it I was nothing.

It's a scary process pointing all the fingers at yourself, not liking what you see and feeling past the point of no return.

Funny thing is when I eventually hit rock bottom it was as if the pressure lifted and everything melted away, like I'd died and let go of everything I once held onto, In that moment I felt reborn.
Not so much a phoenix rising from the ashes, more like a shit stain being flushed from the pan, clearing the way for a fresh start and a new beginning.

Once I'd given my head a good shake I decided to focus on the key factors influencing my current situation, and after assessing the various angles swiftly I came to the conclusion that I'd become a total arsehole, so changing my unhelpful attitude was the first obstacle I needed to overcome.

I decided to slap the pity out of myself and adopt a new attitude which was now going to be one of gratitude, after all I'd made it through the pandemic alive when others hadn't been as fortunate, so why was I feeling sorry for myself.

I decided that looking at my current habits and in particular what I needed to change to affect a positive transformation to my life that would offer the best chance of success moving forward.

The long lost couldn't give a stuff look in the mirror had been replaced by a focussed and intense determined stare that I'd seen so many times throughout my life whenever I'd been a bit lost and dared to challenge myself to be more than I thought I was.

I recall clearly as I stared intensely into my own puffed up tear drenched eyes in the mirror getting very emotional but after a while I could feel a change occurring, and the longer I stared the deeper I looked into my soul, searching for that spark. As I continued to stare a change seemed to be taking place, as if I was morphing, and at some point I saw the real me staring back, and then a voice, direct and hard, "Oh there you are, where the f**k have you been? It's time to get to work."

I once again saw the keen amateur boxer who had trained all his life since he was 12 and who had completed 8 Great North Run half marathons and 2 Liverpool halves. and completed a full marathon at age 42.

Someone who had completed numerous C2C and castles and coast cycle rides since the marathon, and had been a boxing coach, who helped so many in their endeavours and who had ran multiple businesses managing staff and resources prior to the pandemic.

I decided to seek some words of inspiration from YouTube to fuel my recovery.
I happened upon a video with a Dr Jordan Peterson a clinical psychologist from Canada who was making a stand against compelled speech. This poor guy was facing a barrage of abuse and ridicule for his stance from some wet blanket who clearly needed a reality check more than me.

I watched some more and some more and I thought, hang on this is an educated guy, and he's not actually taking a political position he's just taking the view he's not being forced to use speech dictated by the state, and he's way too smart for the people he's facing, who appear to be so locked into their ideology they've stopped thinking for themselves and are just following the prescribed trendy ideologies and propaganda.
The more I watched the more I realised this was no poor guy, this fella is tearing people apart with something that appears to have been lost in society, common sense.

I decided he was making a lot of sense to me so maybe there was a glimmer of hope here, and somehow I've been a bit quick to think I'm going crazy because everyone appears to have lost their collective minds, but they're all still doing better than me so I must be the crazy one, but hey ho let's craic on kimosabi.

The video finishes and I'm feeling more energised and click on to a guy called Joe Rogan and after a while I begin to look a bit deeper.

I'm seeing a struggling comedian and ex martial artist who began a podcast and he's talking to all these different people and he's not trying to be clever he's just being curious and he's again, making sense to me.

So here's someone else I can relate to as I've had my fill of gas telly propaganda doom and gloom news from the paper shuffling Thunderbird puppets.

I move on and click onto my first David Goggins video and my mind is instantly blown.

Suddenly, I am finally awake, and find myself fully switched on by this jacked lunatic talking about how he was fat and how he decided to become a navy seal and the struggles he went through.

I recognised that psycho look in his eyes, a look I had seen so many times in various gyms over the years and I see instantly how driven this guy is, and in that moment I thought " yes, this is more like it."

I decided there and then, "I'm going to start carrying the people carrying the boats and the logs, here we go, strap in because shits about to get real."

"We have lift off!"

I began taking a deeper look at my habits and how I had been prioritising everything in my life.

To my utter embarrassment alcohol and a bad diet had became a primary habit during lockdown, and continued afterwards and I had been making an excuse of being isolated and bored on a night in order to justify my behaviour which had turned me into functioning alcoholic.

Sleep had not been a priority as the alcohol and food were knocking me out for a few hours but I was waking in the middle of the night raging at the world until I finally dozed off.

I'd had no motivation financially as I was dealing with dead people every day and my attitude had been, "well I'm still alive so there's that to be grateful for but I'm 52 so I'll probably not be here much longer anyway and I've had a canny life and completed most things I've wanted to."

Where I grew up expectations had been fairly low and ambitions peaked at gaining a reputation for how many pints of beer you could drink, a body full of tattoos and walking the streets with a hard looking dog and a gold chain wrapped around your neck, while checking in on your 14 kids with 8 different women (I'm exaggerating of course, like I could get 8 women).

I had far surpassed that but now I'm in my 50's and my life had turned into a shower of shit, but a fire was building inside me and I thought, "maybe I can turn this franchise around."
I started to look into videos and books on habits and to be honest my head was like spaghetti as I'm just a simple lad from the North East of England, so paradigms, continuums and synergy and valleys of uncertainty, sounded way above my brain grade.

I thought "balls to that, I need to break this down into simple elements I can understand so it makes sense to me."

I'm stuck in a hole and I feel the books I'm reading are telling me, the size and volume of the hole and what the composition of the soil is, and if I do X, Y and Z then a chemical will be released in my brain which will act as a cue for me to take this or that action, to which I will be rewarded with escape, when all I really need is someone to pass me a stepladder and give me a helping hand out.

I click on another goggins video as this guy has got me stoked and I'm about ready to explode, as a mixture of new found purpose and serious embarrassment coarse through my veins, as I realise that when the pandemic hit, my life had unravelled like a 2 year olds shoelace.

I begin to look at my habits and thought "ok, what are my primary habits?"
In other words "what am I currently prioritising and what effects are they having on my daily life?"

I start writing things down and I quickly discover that everything I am at this moment is a result of me and my attitude towards what I class as my primary habits, secondary habits and occasional activities.

Once I wrote everything down I realised I'd totally lost all focus of the primary habits that had once positively affected my life, and replaced them with some bad habits that were once occasional activities but had over time become regular occurrences and in the long run potentially very harmful.

I set about reprioritising everything and sought to implement my very own Success System for life.

I began my research, and begin to start writing things down and it wasn't long before hours had passed and I had pages of information and ideas were coming at me from all angles.
In my new found drive I thought "easy peasy lemon squeasy".

I began to look at my current habits and began to eliminate the ones having negative effects which meant cutting out alcohol and bad food totally and replacing them with water and eating healthy food. I even cut out tea because I couldn't have a cup without dunking a whole packet of biscuits, so I thought "screw you tea and biscuits."

The gym which had been an occasional activity now became an everyday activity designed to get me into peak physical shape, or at least the fittest 54 year old in my world.

My bad attitude in hating the world was replaced by focusing on humility, gratitude and positivity in order to concentrate on becoming the best version of my 54 year old self.

I also realised I needed new skills as the world had changed, so I began looking into earning multiple income streams from online activities, and education was entered as a primary habit in my system of success.

Next I looked at every one of my relationships and decided the toxic ones had to go, as I realised they were emotionally draining and time consuming and of no use to me as I had no time for negativity. "No time for gossip I'm on a mission!"

I began spending more time around the positive people in my life and cultivating new friendships at the gym in order to focus my mind on gaining positive outcomes from my primary habits.

Gas telly had to go due to the fact it had become a toxic rage triggering relationship, and I no longer resonated on that frequency.

My mind began to clear and over time due to my consistency the weight began to shift, and the more driven, focused and consistent I continued to be the better I felt as the weight began to melt away.

I was adding to my gym friendship group by the day and before I knew it I had made at least a dozen new gym buddies, some of who had their own stories of struggle and I realised then that I wasn't alone.

I stopped focusing on my own personal negative experiences, which made it easier to understand the fact that other people have their own challenges going on in life which to be honest were far worse than that of a 54 year old homeless, penniless, lost soul.
Listening to some people I realised I was doing alright.

My gratitude for life and empathy for others began to increase as I began to form an idea in my mind that I could be helpful to others in some way, and the notes I was continuing to write daily began to take form.

As the weeks passed I lost more weight and my outlook and mindset were picking up by the day.

I was in the gym one day and met this guy, a 24 year old bodybuilder who had wandered into the boxing room just prior to the lockdown and began hitting the bag like a human windmill.

I remember thinking "someone who looks like a Greek god can't be hitting the bag as poorly as that," so I struck up a conversation and he asked if I would coach him. I'd seen him round the gym helping others and I like that, so I agreed. Not that I am anybody, after all I've been hitting a heavy bag for 45 years and never won a round yet, but that's okay I'll keep practicing.

He was the perfect student , he listened, followed instruction and was totally focused on improving himself.
I took this as a sign that I was meant to give something back.
As the time went by he began to open up.
Then one day he told me his story and I found myself welling up. He showed me a picture of when he was in hospital some years back suffering with diabetes and really poorly and all skin and bone. When he was well enough to be released he decided to do a bit weights to build his body back up as he was so weak and he'd managed to stick to it and here eight years later he looked like a Greek God.
Thing is, thats all people see, this flawless Greek god walking round the gym like that's all he's ever been. Not the poorly lad in hospital suffering and fighting for his life.

As our workouts became more frequent we began to discuss his life plan (he writes everything down) gym record, career aspirations, financial dreams and wealth aspirations, developing new skills (learning Spanish) and working on relationships. I remember laughing at what seemed like 5 minutes ago I was drunk shouting at the telly, and now i'm coaching and offering life advice to this monster in the gym (well at least discussing things he may wish to think about avoiding in order to progress and continue on his journey of success).

Something had occurred to me one day at the gym as I was chatting with my new friendship group (there was 6 of us and we had all got to know one another at this point), In no other setting would I have engaged with these young men.
Here we are connecting through boxing and life discussions in a gym setting, which if I'm honest is one of only a few places I've ever really felt alive and at home.

For me as a 54-year-old ex amateur boxer and coach the gym has always acted as an avenue to learn as well as share some hard-earned wisdom. Now I find myself guiding the younger men to critically think for themselves and work through life's ups and downs, offering insights on career, relationships, and personal growth, and we always have a right good laugh.

My hope is that these young men will gain from my coaching and mentorship, learning from my seasoned experiences
(or at least what not to do) which will hopefully help them gain perspective and better navigate some of life's never ending roller coaster of often complex challenges.

I do tend to think the physicality of boxing which strengthens both mind and body, promotes discipline, focus, and camaraderie, may add other dimensions to their characters.

I have found that the gym has allowed the intergenerational bond we have formed, to overcome the age barrier, creating quite a solid connection that I feel does enrich understanding, respect, and personal growth, which as far as I can tell is much needed in this modern world where young men struggle to find role models. Not that I have ever thought of myself as a role model but at 54 years of age I can certainly speak of my experiences and offer insights into what challenges young people may face and discuss options to consider and potential routes forward.

Having spoken with many young people just setting out in adult life the questions comes around as to what they want to do and I've thought about this a lot and come to the conclusion that the question is not just , "What do you want to do with your life?" The question is also, "How do you want your life to look?"

Answering a personal calling is akin to uncovering the roadmap to personal fulfilment. This is something I have struggled with most of my life as I've bumped and bashed my way attempting to overcome the many obstacles life has thrown my way (as we all do).

I am beginning to understand that a persons calling isn't just a profession; it is an energy force that aligns ones passions, strengths, and values, and embracing it isn't merely about choosing a path but living authentically.

I believe ones purpose hides within this alignment, fostering a sense of meaning that has the potential to transcend the day to day boring and mundane. I also think if one ignores this it often leads to a lingering sense of being unfulfilled.

It's in heeding this call that the pursuit of purpose gains momentum, steering one towards a life of resonance and impact and by answering a calling, one has the ability to find real purpose in the very essence of who they are.

I recall listening to Bruce Lee once taking about hacking away at the unessential until the truth is revealed, reflecting the idea that self-improvement is more about uncovering and refining one's innate qualities, rather than just adding something entirely new.

As I continued to scrutinise my life and break it down into simplicity, i realised there was three elements always at play that could tip the scales of life at any time.
Primary habits, secondary habits and occasional activities.

Regaining focus on my primary habits, I realised these were always the foundational elements that had unconsciously produced the greatest results throughout my life

These habits constituted the essential rituals that once defined my life, from my first days, anchoring my routines and influencing my well-being, offering balance to my growth and development.

Secondary habits, while not as fundamental, added depth and variation.

Occasional activities connected everything by introducing moments of novelty and delight, but their sporadic nature offered both surprise and unpredictability.

Together, these three layers had been largely responsible for my human experience, each contributing its distinct advantages and drawbacks, ultimately crafting the unique patterns that had composed my life.

I decided to take a deeper dive into them as I continued to write everything down and draw it all together as my success system for life began to solidify.

As I continued with this exercise I began to see things that appeared clear and obvious when I looked around at the people I knew I started to piece a few things together.

I knew someone who was successful in earning money but was constantly switched on and had trouble sleeping, which resulted in them forever moaning about how tired they were and how much things cost, because they spent it as soon as they got it, as they had to have the best of everything.
This person couldn't hold a relationship down and self medicated with alcohol, was overweight and had bad eating habits and was too busy to go to the gym and always said they just didn't have time.

I knew another person who had healthy eating habits but struggled financially who was always commenting they couldn't get a good nights sleep due to money worries and didn't have the energy to go to the gym.

I knew another who had a high status job but socialised most nights, drank a lot of alcohol, smoked and was severely overweight and onto his second wife and family.

What I began to realise was that everyone I knew was successful in some areas but not so much others and it was as if they had sacrificed some habits for the glory of a few, mostly financial (although for some not in an intelligent way).
For example, the willingness to give up sleep and quality family time and a healthy lifestyle in order to socialise and position themselves for promotion and status and money.

From this exercise I formulated a list of habits one by one and in doing so pulled all the ideas I had been writing down and formulate a system of success that would carry me through the rest of my life.

Chapter 1

The Magnificent Seven

The Magnificent Seven

Once I had wrote everything down and dissected it all I put it into my habit system formula and prioritised each habit in order, something quite extraordinary happened.

Firstly I counted seven habits which I labelled The Magnificent Seven and set them out and listed them in a certain order, not of Importance as they were each as important as the next.
it was more about how they unfolded on the journey of human development.

I wanted to imprint them on my mind and in looking at them I realised the first letters clearly spelled out SHEER FW. Now I knew what it was going to take to succeed, SHEER FOCUSED WORK.

I was so excited I began to question and scrutinise each one and in doing so I began to look back over time to see if the ancients had left any clues and what I discovered took me to a whole other level as I realised the number Seven held great meaning across the ages.

The Power of Seven the ancient symbol of balance and harmony A Universal Code for Success
Numbers have fascinated humanity since the dawn of civilisation. From the earliest scholars of ancient Mesopotamia to the most brilliant minds of today, patterns, sequences, and numerical mysteries have shaped our understanding of the world. Among all the numbers that hold symbolic and practical significance, one stands out above the rest: the number Seven.

Seven is woven into the fabric of history, nature, and human achievement. It is a number that has captivated philosophers, mathematicians, religious leaders, and scientists alike. It is a number that seems to whisper to us across the ages, inviting us to uncover its secrets. The truth is, the number seven is not just another arbitrary figure, it is a blueprint for balance, excellence, and mastery.

When you begin to recognise the power of seven in the world around you, patterns emerge that are too profound to ignore.

The Power of Seven

- **Seven notes in a musical scale.** Every piece of music that has ever moved your soul is built on a foundational seven-note sequence (do, re, mi, fa, sol, la, ti). The moment we reach the eighth note, we return to the beginning, an octave higher, but still built upon the same fundamental pattern.
- **Seven colors in the rainbow.** Nature itself adheres to the power of seven. When light refracts, it reveals the full spectrum in precisely seven colors: red, orange, yellow, green, blue, indigo, and violet. This is the universal signature of visible light, a reminder that even beauty and perception are governed by this sacred number.
- **Seven days in a week.** The entire world organises its time according to a seven-day cycle. Civilisations across continents and centuries, from the Babylonians to the modern age, have adhered to this structure, recognising its natural rhythm and flow.
- **Seven continents.** Our planet itself is divided into seven vast landmasses, shaping the movement of civilisations, cultures, and history.
- **Seven wonders of the ancient world.** Even in antiquity, humanity acknowledged the magic of seven when selecting the most awe-inspiring monuments of creativity and engineering.
- **Seven chakras.** In Eastern traditions, the human body is believed to have seven primary energy centers, each essential to spiritual and physical well-being.
- **Seven deadly sins, seven virtues.** Religious and philosophical teachings recognise the power of seven as a framework for human morality, guiding individuals toward enlightenment or downfall.

When you step back and truly see how often this number appears in the systems that govern our reality, you begin to understand that the number seven is not a coincidence, it is a fundamental principle. It is as if the universe itself has given us a formula for balance, growth, and success.
But what if you could harness this universal power and apply it to your own life?
What if, instead of seeing seven as a mystical curiosity, you embraced it as a practical system for your very own success?

This book is about more than just observing the power of seven, it is about *mastering* it. The Ultimate Success System For Life is a carefully structured foundational framework that will help you track your own personal success, empowering you to live your best life.

History is littered with stories of greatness, and those who achieve remarkable success often follow a structured approach, whether consciously or unconsciously. The key to lasting success is not luck, talent, or sheer willpower alone. It is about understanding the fundamental principles that govern achievement, balance, and fulfilment.

By following this system you will be able to live and understand your own personalised blueprint for success, one that aligns with the universal laws of growth and mastery. Whether you want to achieve financial independence, cultivate deep and meaningful relationships, master your craft, or unlock the highest version of yourself, this system will provide the solid foundation to make it happen.

Imagine having a guiding framework that simplifies decision-making, maximises productivity, and ensures that every step you take moves you closer to your dreams. Imagine unlocking the same power that nature, time, music, and wisdom have relied upon for millennia.

This book is your invitation to embark on that journey.

But before you turn the page, I want you to do something. I want you to open your mind to the possibility that you are standing at the threshold of something life-changing. You are about to discover a system that has the power to elevate every aspect of your existence.

The Ultimate Success System For Life is more than just learning a new philosophy, it is about stepping into your full potential.

Are you ready?

Then let us dive in!

Sleep

"Sleep is the golden chain that ties health and our bodies together." - Thomas Dekker

Thomas Dekker's quote emphasises the vital link between sleep, health, and overall well-being. Picture sleep as a golden chain, intricately connecting different aspects of our physical and mental health. Just as a chain holds together various links, a good night's sleep binds our body's functions, allowing for proper restoration, rejuvenation, and the maintenance of optimal health. This metaphor underscores the essential role sleep plays in supporting the delicate balance necessary for our bodies to function at their best.

Sleep is your ultimate secret weapon and the body and mind's healer, influencing both mental and physical well-being profoundly.
The brain consolidates memories, enhancing learning and cognitive functions.
Emotionally, it regulates your mood, fostering resilience and a positive outlook.
Physically, sleep revitalises your body, bolstering the immune system, regulating hormones, and promoting cellular repair. Adequate rest aids in weight management, lowering the risk of chronic diseases like diabetes and heart conditions.

Overall, the quality of your sleep rejuvenates, enhancing focus, creativity, and decision-making while reducing stress and enhancing your overall physical health, making it an essential component for your balanced, thriving life.

I want you to reset your mind to think "My greatest days begin with a good nights sleep".

Health & Nutrition

Let food be thy medicine and medicine be thy food." — *Hippocrates*, the Father of Modern Medicine

Hippocrates' timeless quote shows clearly the powerful connection between what we eat and how we feel. Nutrition plays a central role in maintaining physical and mental health, preventing disease, and promoting longevity. Adopting a healthy and nutritious lifestyle is more than just a dietary choice, it's a lifelong investment in one's overall well-being.

One of your most immediate advantages of a nutritious lifestyle is improved physical health. Consuming a balanced diet provides you with essential vitamins and minerals that your body needs to function optimally. These nutrients support your immune system, regulate hormones, strengthen bones, and improve digestion.
Maintaining a healthy diet also significantly reduces your risk of chronic diseases as you age over time.

Nutrition doesn't only influence your physical health, it has profound effects on mental and emotional well-being as there are strong links between diet and mood.
Furthermore, balanced eating habits can stabilise your mood swings and improve your focus and energy levels. Nutritious meals can help you feel more alert, calm, and emotionally balanced throughout the day.

Adopting a healthy lifestyle also enhances your overall quality of life. When eating well you will be more motivated to exercise, get adequate sleep, and avoid harmful behaviours like smoking or excessive alcohol consumption. These lifestyle choices reinforce one another, creating a positive feedback loop that supports your long-term health and happiness.
Remember, nothing tastes as good as being fit and healthy feels.

Exercise

Those who think they have no time for exercise will sooner or later have to find time for illness." — *Edward Stanley*, 19th-century British statesman

Edward Stanley's quote is a powerful reminder of the long-term consequences of neglecting physical activity. It highlights a simple truth: prioritising regular exercise today prevents major health issues tomorrow.
Making time for physical activity, even just 30 minutes a day yields countless benefits. It strengthens the heart, builds muscle, supports joint health, and boosts metabolism. People who exercise regularly are at significantly lower risk for chronic conditions like heart disease, obesity, type 2 diabetes, and osteoporosis.

For you, the benefits don't stop at the body. Exercise also improves your brain health. Exercise increases blood flow to your brain, enhances your memory and concentration, and promotes the growth of new brain cells. It has been shown to reduce symptoms of depression and anxiety and improve overall mood through the release of endorphins and other "feel-good" chemicals.
In today's busy world, it's easy to say, "I don't have time." But as Stanley warns, neglecting exercise often leads to poor health, which can cost you far more time, money, and energy in the long run. Hospital visits, medications, surgeries, and lost productivity can all result from a sedentary lifestyle.

The truth is simple: making exercise a priority is an act of prevention for you. It is an investment in your health, energy, and longevity. As this quote suggests, the choice is not whether to make time but *when* you will be forced to. The wise decision is to act now so make the space in your life and get moving.

Education

Education is the most powerful weapon which you can use to change the world." - Nelson Mandela.

Nelson Mandela's powerful statement underscores the transformative impact of education on both individuals and societies. Education serves as a catalyst for change, empowering individuals with knowledge, critical thinking skills, and a broader perspective on the world. When armed with education, individuals gain the ability to challenge injustices, break barriers, and contribute meaningfully to positive societal shifts.

A lifelong commitment to learning amplifies your personal growth across every facet of your life.
Continuous education sharpens cognitive abilities, fostering adaptability, critical thinking, and problem-solving skills.
Education enriches perspectives, nurturing curiosity and creativity.
Remaining abreast of new information and technologies ensures relevance in a rapidly evolving world.

Lifelong learning broadens your career prospects, enabling career advancement and professional fulfilment.
Education cultivates your resilience by embracing change and new challenges confidently.
Moreover, ongoing education enriches your relationships, fostering empathy and understanding diverse viewpoints.
Embracing continuous learning becomes a cornerstone for your self-improvement, contributing not just to personal success but also to societal progress and innovation.

In an ever changing world you are never too old or too young to learn something new (especially about yourself).

Relationships

"The quality of your life is the quality of your relationships." - Tony Robbins.

Tony Robbins emphasises that the richness of life hinges on the quality of relationships. Positive connections contribute to joy, fulfillment, and a sense of belonging. It's not solely about personal achievements; rather, it's the shared experiences and emotional support from relationships that elevate the human experience and create a fulfilling life.

Your positive relationships serve as a dynamic source of energy and tranquility, balancing your emotional well-being.
They provide unwavering support, fostering resilience during challenges while also celebrating successes. Such connections ignite enthusiasm, offering motivation and encouragement to pursue aspirations.

In moments of distress, they provide you with a comforting sanctuary, easing stress and anxiety.
Constructive relationships promote your personal growth through shared experiences, diverse perspectives, and mutual learning. They cultivate a sense of belonging and acceptance, nurturing mental stability and happiness.

Ultimately, these bonds create a harmonious equilibrium, energising you during action and offering you solace during moments of repose, enriching your life, with enduring fulfilment.

Remember, the test of true friendship is not when things in your life are going right, but when you face hard times, then you find out exactly who your friends are, the ride or die, the solid advice, the ear you can bend without judgement.

Financial Intelligence

"Financial literacy is not just about money; it's about empowerment, freedom, and creating the life you want." - Robert Kiyosaki.

Robert Kiyosaki's quote highlights the profound impact of financial literacy beyond mere monetary understanding. Consider financial literacy as a key that unlocks doors to empowerment and freedom. When individuals possess the knowledge and skills to navigate financial matters, they gain the ability to make informed decisions, manage resources wisely, and shape their financial destinies.

Your Financial literacy and intelligence will empower you to navigate the complex landscape of personal finance adeptly. Understanding concepts like multiple income streams, budgeting, investing, and debt management fosters informed decision-making, leading you to the path of financial stability and security.

Financial intelligence cultivates responsible spending habits, ensuring you have a balanced financial life.
Enhanced financial intelligence allows you to set and achieve long-term goals, whether it's homeownership, retirement planning, or entrepreneurial pursuits and mitigates risks, creating a safety net during economic uncertainties.

Moreover, financial literacy enables you to pass on valuable knowledge to future generations, fostering a cycle of financial well-being and prosperity, ultimately granting you the freedom to pursue your dreams and aspirations.

Remember, when it comes to money, it's better to have it and not need it, than to need it and not have it. When you see someone rushing around shouting "time is money" think to yourself, "money is time and freedom".

Work

"The only way to do great work is to love what you do." - Steve Jobs,

Steve Jobs quote encapsulates the essence of achieving greatness through passion and dedication. When you genuinely love what you do, work transcends mere obligation; it becomes a source of inspiration and purpose. Passion fuels innovation, perseverance, and the commitment to surpass conventional boundaries, ultimately leading to the creation of impactful and extraordinary work.

Your work instills discipline, structure, and purpose into your life. It cultivates a strong ethic, enhancing your productivity and focus.
Consistent engagement in meaningful tasks nurtures your expertise and proficiency, fostering your personal and professional growth.

Moreover, a habitual approach to work instills resilience, teaching adaptability in the face of the many challenges life may throw at you at any given time.
Work creates a rhythm that helps balance your life, offering a sense of achievement and satisfaction.

Furthermore, it establishes a routine conducive to your time management, enabling you to better grasp priorities.
Ultimately, embracing your work nurtures skills, resilience, and a fulfilling sense of accomplishment, enriching your life in many ways.

Work is not just a job, it doesn't matter where you are in life and at what stage, with your system in place, it is through action and work that will lead you to wherever it is you want to go.

Chapter 2

**Primary Habits
Secondary Habits
&
Occasional Activities**

The ultimate success system for life is based on the foundational magnificent seven primary habits.

There has to be more to life though and other habits that add variety and depth. These we will term secondary habits and occasional activities, and there are pros and cons to each.

Primary habits

Pros.

On the positive side, these habits reinforce one another: good sleep, nutrition, and exercise improve physical and mental performance; education keeps the mind sharp and adaptable; relationships provide emotional support; financial intelligence builds security and freedom; and meaningful work gives structure and purpose.

Together, they reduce stress, prevent disease, enhance resilience, and increase life satisfaction. Over time, these habits compound, creating long-term well-being, stability, and personal growth.

Cons.

Pursuing all seven consistently also comes with challenges. They require significant time, energy, and discipline, which can create pressure or feelings of failure if balance isn't achieved. Overemphasis on one area, such as work or fitness can undermine another area like sleep or relationships. Nutrition and fitness can be costly or confusing; financial learning may feel overwhelming; and maintaining relationships demands emotional investment. In striving for perfection across all seven, people risk burnout or guilt when falling short.

To sum up, the Magnificent Seven provide a powerful framework for success, but the key lies in balance, flexibility, and sustainable progress rather than rigid perfection, in other words enjoy and understand each step of your journey but don't beat yourself up about it.

Secondary Habits
Pros:
Secondary habits encompass activities like hobbies, socialising, reading, or learning new skills.

These habits add colour to life, fostering creativity, social connections, and personal development.

Engaging in hobbies promotes relaxation, reduces stress, and offers an outlet for self-expression and exploration.

Building habits around learning new skills or pursuing interests outside of work broadens perspectives, stimulates the mind, and often leads to a more fulfilled and balanced life.

Cons:
While secondary habits contribute positively to life, excessive focus on these activities might lead to mismanagement of time, causing neglect of the magnificent seven habits and responsibilities or self-care.

Occasional Activities

Pros:
Occasional activities, such as going out drinking and socialising with friends ,eating takeaway food, traveling, attending events, or spontaneous adventures etc inject spontaneity and excitement into life.

They provide memorable experiences, broaden horizons, and offer opportunities for relaxation and rejuvenation.

These activities break the routine, stimulate creativity, and often result in new perspectives, personal growth, and cherished memories.

Cons:
While occasional activities enrich life experiences, their sporadic nature can sometimes disrupt routine, leading to inconsistency in helpful habits.

Excessive indulgence in occasional activities might also strain financial resources or lead to a lack of focus on long-term goals if not balanced with moderation.

There may also be a danger that these occasional habits, if not moderated, could take hold and become primary habits.

I had found this out to my detriment without even realising what had happened.

I concluded that in order to effect transformational life changes, a thorough understanding and a well-balanced approach to my primary habits, secondary habits, and occasional activities were going to be pivotal.

I now knew the magnificent seven primary habits provided me stability and structure, whereas my secondary habits and occasional activities may add some depth and richness to life if managed in moderation.

Responsibility and prioritisation, and mindful management of time and space were going to be crucial to ensure that my habits and activities complemented each other and affected the transformational change I was focused on.

Balancing these elements were going to allow me to enjoy the benefits of routine while exploring new experiences and avenues for personal growth and happiness.

Upon reflection, I recognised that for my success system to truly thrive, meticulous attention to each of the magnificent seven habits was imperative. Any deviation from alignment carried the risk of disrupting my life's balance and potentially triggering a derailing and negative trajectory.

I began to look at what could possibly distract me and derail my success system for life.

Chapter 3

Distractions

Distractions

"The successful warrior is the average man, with laser-like focus."
- Bruce Lee

Bruce Lee's quote highlights the transformative power of unwavering focus. It suggests that success isn't reserved for the extraordinary; rather, it emerges from the ordinary person who channels their energy with precision. By maintaining laser-like focus amid distractions, one can harness their potential and navigate the path to success with clarity and purpose.

I was acutely aware that when the Pandemic hit and the world stopped and everyone was locked down, that things were going to be bad.
Exactly how bad and to what end in the long term nobody knew at the time.

What I did know is that this was going to be a time of major distractions from the routine of daily life that we were all used to. When the restrictions finally eased the return to "normal life" was anything but normal.
I carried on piecing together my success system and decided to explore in detail the different everyday habits that can distract anyone from their life's focus.

To my astonishment I realised that the world we now live in has so many distractions in place that it can become quite easy to lose focus on positive habits due to the allure of these distractions.

Mobile Phones

"I fear the day that technology will surpass our human interaction. The world will have a generation of idiots." - Albert Einstein

Albert Einstein's quote reflects concerns about the potential consequences of technology on human interaction. He expresses a fear that as technology advances, there's a risk of diminishing genuine human connections. The term "generation of idiots" suggests a worry that over reliance on technology might lead to a decline in meaningful communication and interpersonal skills, emphasising the importance of mindful and balanced use of mobile phones in our lives.

Smartphones have admittedly revolutionised communication, offering unparalleled connectivity and convenience. On the positive side, they enhance productivity, enabling quick access to information, work emails, and organisation tools.
Smartphones also facilitate social interaction, bridging distances with video calls and social media.

However, their constant accessibility often leads to distractions, impacting focus and mental health.
Notifications, social media, and addictive apps contribute to decreased attention spans and increased stress.
Excessive screen time may lead to physical issues like eye strain and poor posture.
While smartphones offer immense benefits, managing their use is crucial to balance their advantages with potential distractions and health concerns.

Social Media

"The downside of social media is that it's made too many of you comfortable with disrespecting people and not getting punched in the mouth for it." - Ice T

Ice T brings awareness to the downside of social media, noting it fosters a comfort with disrespect due to the lack of immediate consequences. The absence of face-to-face interactions diminishes accountability, emphasising the need for responsible behavior to maintain respectful discourse and counteract negative trends on these platforms.

Social media, while a tool for connection, often becomes a vortex of distraction, diverting attention from one's personal life goals. The addictive nature of social media consumes valuable time, fragmenting focus and productivity.

Endless scrolling may lead to unrealistic comparisons, sowing seeds of self-doubt and detracting from personal progress.
The curated content often portrays an unrealistic view, leading to misplaced priorities and a skewed sense of success.

Constant notifications disrupt concentration, hindering deep work essential for goal attainment.
Moreover, excessive screen time diminishes real-world interactions, impacting relationships and personal development. Succumbing to its allure can deviate us from pursuing personal aspirations, diluting our focus and impeding progress towards fulfilling life objectives.

Television

"I find television very educational. Every time someone turns it on, I go in the other room and read a book." - Groucho Marx

Groucho Marx's lighthearted remark on television suggests a witty perspective on its educational value. By humorously implying that he opts for reading over watching, Marx playfully challenges the notion that television is the primary source of education. The quote encourages a lighthearted reflection on the balance between entertainment and intellectual pursuits in the era of television.

Television, while entertaining, poses a significant distraction, impeding progress towards life goals.
Binge-watching consumes vast amounts of time, diverting focus from productive endeavors and personal growth.

Its passive nature fosters sedentary habits, impacting physical health and vitality.
Excessive TV viewing diminishes motivation and drive, often replacing active pursuits with inertia.

Content absorption can skew perceptions of reality, shaping aspirations based on fictional narratives rather than personal ambitions.
Moreover, habitual viewing erodes valuable time that could be channelled into skill development or goal-oriented tasks.

Surrendering to prolonged television consumption undermines the pursuit of dreams, diluting focus and hindering progress towards life's meaningful objectives.

Gossip

"Great minds discuss ideas; average minds discuss events; small minds discuss people." - Eleanor Roosevelt

Eleanor Roosevelt's insightful quote delves into the hierarchy of conversational topics. By categorising discussions into great minds focusing on ideas, average minds on events, and small minds on people, she highlights the potential pitfalls of gossip. It encourages us to elevate our conversations, emphasising the value of discussing substantial and meaningful subjects over indulging in superficial or negative chatter.

Engaging in gossip derails progress towards personal goals by diverting energy and focus and fosters a negative environment, consuming valuable time that could be invested in self-improvement or goal pursuits.

Gossiping breeds distrust and strains relationships, impacting collaborations vital for advancement.
It sows seeds of negativity, derailing positive thinking and stifling personal growth.
Involvement in gossip often leads to conflicts, sidetracking attention from productive endeavors.

Moreover, it undermines credibility and damages reputation, hindering professional advancements.
Giving into the lure of gossip disrupts focus, depletes energy, and fosters an environment of distraction, impeding progress towards achieving meaningful life goals.

Toxic Relationships

"Sometimes we're so desperate for love that we ignore the red flags. But toxic relationships drain you emotionally; it's crucial to recognise when the cost of staying outweighs the benefits." - Steve Maraboli

Maraboli's quote highlights our tendency to prioritise love, often disregarding warning signs in relationships. Desperation blinds us to red flags, leading to toxic dynamics. It urges self-respect and awareness to prevent harm, emphasising the importance of prioritising personal well-being over the pursuit of companionship.

Toxic relationships act as a significant impediment to life goals by draining emotional resources and creating turmoil.
They breed negativity, fostering self-doubt and diminishing confidence, hindering personal growth, as such connections demand excessive emotional labour, diverting attention from pursuing aspirations.

Toxic relationships often lead to conflicts and stress, disrupting focus and mental clarity essential for goal achievement.
They erode self-worth, impeding decision-making and inhibiting risk-taking crucial for progress.

Moreover, these relationships consume time and energy better invested in constructive endeavors.
Toxic bonds hamper progress, destabilise emotional well-being, and obstruct the path towards realising one's full potential and life objectives.

News

"Listening to the news is like navigating a river. It provides the current of knowledge, shaping our understanding of the world. Yet, be cautious of its rapids – sensationalism and bias. Stay vigilant, choose your sources wisely, and let the flow of information enrich, not drown, your perspective." - Diane Sawyer

Sawyers words make us aware that misinformation and bias can mislead. She highlights the need for caution and critical thinking to navigate the news effectively and discern reality from distortion.

News inundated with propaganda often hijacks focus, diverting attention from personal aspirations.
Biased reporting skews perspectives, fostering fear, and anxiety, hindering clarity and forward momentum.
Excessive exposure to manipulated information disrupts critical thinking, clouding judgment, and altering priorities.

Constant consumption of sensationalised news hijacks mental space, inducing stress and worry, reducing the mental bandwidth needed for goal pursuit.
Moreover, falling victim to biased narratives drains time that could otherwise be utilised for self-improvement or goal-oriented endeavors.

Succumbing to manipulated news cycles fragments focus, sows confusion, and impedes progress towards achieving meaningful life goals.

Cigarettes and Vapes

Freedom from nicotine addiction is the greatest gift you can give yourself." - Allen Carr

Cigarettes and vapes act as a pervasive distraction, compromising health and derailing life goals.
Addiction to smoking and vaping consumes time, money, and energy, diverting focus from personal aspirations.

Health issues arising from smoking and vaping weaken vitality, hampering progress and hindering the pursuit of fulfilling life objectives.

Alcohol

"Drinking makes you forget, but it doesn't erase the consequences. It's a temporary escape with a lasting toll. The highs are fleeting, and the lows can be profound. Choose clarity over the fog of intoxication; it's in sobriety that we truly face and conquer life's challenges." - Carrie Fisher

Alcohol misuse disrupts focus and impairs judgment, derailing life goals.
Excessive drinking absorbs time and resources, hindering productivity and clarity.
Health repercussions and addiction issues arising from alcohol consumption divert attention from personal aspirations, compromising progress towards fulfilling life objectives.

Unhealthy Eating

"Every time you eat or drink, you are either feeding disease or fighting it." - Heather Morgan

Heather Morgan's quote stresses the significance of dietary choices in health. It conveys the idea that every meal is a pivotal moment, influencing whether we nourish the body or contribute to disease. By recognizing the connection between nutrition and well-being, it urges individuals to make mindful and health-conscious eating decisions for long-term vitality.

Frequent reliance on takeaway foods disrupts healthy habits, impacting energy and well-being.
Unhealthy eating habits drain finances and compromise physical health, diverting focus from personal goals.
The time spent ordering and consuming takeout detracts from pursuits towards a balanced and fulfilling lifestyle.

Nights Out

"Endless nights of socialising may seem like a thrilling escape, but in the relentless pursuit of pleasure, the essence of life's depth may be lost. Remember, balance is the art of a fulfilling existence; excessive revelry can overshadow the subtler, meaningful moments that truly enrich our lives." - Robin Sharma

Frequent nights out disrupt routines and deplete energy, hindering progress towards life goals.
Late nights impact productivity and mental clarity, affecting focus on personal aspirations.

Shopping

"Shopping can be a delightful pastime, but when it becomes a compulsive pursuit, it masks deeper needs with fleeting acquisitions. The joy of possessions fades, leaving an emptiness that no amount of purchases can fill. Find contentment beyond the checkout, for true wealth lies in a fulfilled heart, not a filled closet." - Ellen Goodman

Frequent shopping indulgences divert resources and attention from life goals.
Impulsive spending drains finances and time, impacting progress towards aspirations.

Compulsive shopping habits erode focus and discipline, hindering the pursuit of meaningful achievements and personal growth.
summing this up I realised our hyper-connected world, with all of these modern distractions like social media, constant notifications, and an overflow of information divert our attention.

They fragment our focus, leading to stress, reduced productivity, and neglect of essential aspects like exercise, relaxation, and meaningful connections, ultimately impacting our health and well-being detrimentally.

National Health Service (NHS), Mental Health Foundation, and reports published by organisations like Mind and the Office for National Statistics (ONS) in the UK, Indicate about 1 in 4 individuals are experiencing a mental health issue each year.

Chapter 4

Making the change

Making the Change

"The secret of change is to focus all of your energy not on fighting the old, but on building the new." - Socrates

In this insightful quote attributed to Socrates, the essence of making a positive life change or transformation is beautifully encapsulated. Socrates encourages a forward-looking approach, advising that the key to change lies in directing one's energy toward creating something new rather than dwelling on the past. By emphasising the constructive aspect of change, the quote inspires individuals to channel their efforts into building a better, more fulfilling future, fostering a mindset of growth, resilience, and optimism.

With this insight I decided to take a look at how my personal habit system looked prior to taking action.

Primary habits
Job, Gossip, Toxic relationships, Alcohol,
Takeaway food, Television, News

Secondary habits
Sleep.

Occasional activities
Positive relationships, Exercise, Education, Finances, Healthy eating.

As you can see it was a shower of shite, or "une pluie de merde", as the French would say.

How it looks now following the Magnificent Seven habits in the ultimate success system for life.

Primary habits
Sleep, Health & Nutrition, Exercise, Education, Relationships, Financial Intelligence, Work.

Secondary habits
Reading, Educational videos, New ventures. Meeting new people, discussing ideas.

Occasional activity
Takeaway food, Socialising,

It's hard to imagine something as simple as this could have such a transformational affect, but for me it did. No gas telly, no Fakebook, no alcohol, no gossip, no toxic relationships.
Writing all this down had reignited the drive I had in me all along. Constantly referring to it maintained my focus and day by day things got better.

I began to get fitter as I lost weight, and my outlook continued to improve as I had surrounded myself with positive people, and was focusing more on the future as I continued to work on my ultimate success system for life.

Following this system enabled me to become more disciplined, efficient, consistent and more productive, while also making me more accountable which helped maintain my drive and focus.
My clothes were falling off me and I was able to put the tents I'd been wearing out to pasture as in 9 months I had shed over 3 stone in weight.
This was just the beginning as my transformation continued.

Transformation

"Transformation is not a future event, it's a present activity. Don't resist it; embrace the process, and you'll find the strength and joy of becoming who you are meant to be." - Eckhart Tolle

Eckhart Tolle's insight on transformation highlights its immediate nature, not a distant event but a present, ongoing process. He urges acceptance over resistance, emphasising that embracing change unlocks strength and joy. This perspective encourages a mindful engagement with life's evolution, fostering personal development and alignment with one's authentic self.

Positive changes stem from intentional actions and mindset shifts and my thoughts were now clear and purposeful. As long as I continued to focus on my Magnificent Seven Primary Habits then I continued to see results.

Consistency is the key element to the system as it sustains my momentum, builds mastery, and minimises setbacks and assures my long term success.
I practice gratitude, focusing on what's present rather than dwelling on shortcomings.
I embrace change with adaptability, staying open to new experiences.

I reflect on past experiences, learning from both successes and setbacks.
Through drive and commitment, resilience, and a consistent proactive approach, my success system for life will arm me with whatever life throws my way.

I now felt in a position to start setting some goals.

Goals

A word on goals
Winners and losers both have goals, but the distinction lies in execution.
Winners persist, adapt, learn from failures, and maintain consistency despite setbacks.

Losers on the other hand might lack perseverance, succumb to obstacles, or abandon their goals prematurely as happens in the month of January most years when people utter the immortal phrase "New year new me", then 3 weeks later find their brains mumbling "different year same shit" as their enthusiasm is abandoned and they go back to the way they always were (I have a theory on this as to the reason this fails, it could be due to the resolution being an add on and not a replacement, where people focus on time instead of creating space).

The mindset, resilience, and perseverance of winners ultimately differentiates them from those who fail to achieve their goals.

Losers can however become winners through introspection, embracing failure as a learning tool and taking action.
If one learns to cultivate resilience, while adjusting strategies, to develop a growth mindset, then one can persevere despite challenges.

I believe that is why the ultimate success system for life works, it's not a plan, it's not about being motivated, it's about connection and balance of one's self, whilst managing tempting distractions.

Prioritising personal integrity, consistency, honing skills and fostering discipline, to stay adaptable, and maintain a relentless dedication to improvement and a purposeful life is the ultimate goal.

For everyone this is a personal internal, physical, emotional and mental transformation and it is for ones self alone, it is not to please others or seek validation.

Another thing to remember, losing is just a matter of giving up, as winning is just a matter of carrying on when you really want to give up.

Winners and Losers

Thinking about winners reminds me of a scene out of the movie The Rock (1996)

Sean Connery plays an hardened British Secret Service Agent and Nicolas Cages who plays an FBI Chemical Weapons Specialist with no experience in combat situations, are preparing to battle forces that have taken over Alcatraz, when Connery"s character asks Cage "are you sure you're ready for this?"

Cage replies " I'll do my best."

Connery responds with a menacing look " Your best? Losers always whine about their best, winners go home with the prom queen." (or words to that affect).

Cage replies "Carla was the prom queen."

Connery looking surprised asks "Really?"

Cage cocks his gun and with a steel eyed gaze, replies "Yeah!"

The message for me is that there's a success monster lurking inside everyone, ready for action at a moments notice should they be ready to rise to the call and become their own hero.

As Dr Jordan Peterson said " You should become a monster, then you should learn to control it."

As I pondered Peterson's words I thought " Ok, it's time to release your inner monster and become the best most limitless version of you, and it's only took 54 years to realise".

The Limitless Epiphany

I watch a lot of movies, I think it comes from my younger days when I would go to the morning matinee at the local cinema and watch Sinbad movies and escape into a world of magic and adventure. The feeling has never left me but nowadays I play a different game and look for the hidden meanings in movies.

Limitless (2011) is one such movie that centres on the Bradley Cooper character Eddie Morra, a struggling writer who has lost motivation and his girlfriend ends their relationship and he suffers from writers block. Eddie bumps into his ex brother in law who gives him a mysterious clear pill which clears his mind and makes him insanely productive.
It was while watching the movie something clicked and I instantly had to go back and rewatch the movie.

As I followed the movie everything I was working on instantly presented itself in the movie and I realised it wasn't the pill that transformed Eddies life, it was the following.

Eddie gets a good night sleep and the next day cleans his room thereby removing all the distractions and obstacles and excuses that had been in his way as he began to take responsibility and put his life in order.

Once he cleared and ordered his room suddenly the writers block evaporated and he completed his book in 4 days. Eddie steps out into the street and his whole perspective changes, he addressed his appearance, hair cut and new suit. Eddie begins to exercise and learn a new language. Next thing Eddie did was create a new social circle of positive people which boosted his confidence and he began to live life and take action in order to move forward. He then becomes a trader and after leaping off a cliff comes up with a big idea.
It was at this stage I saw the hidden meaning (or maybe I'm just see things differently now, either way it was having an effect).

As I sat transfixed a thought entered my head and my brain went into overdrive as I realised It was not the pill that was having such a positive effect, it was Eddies system of habits.
Sleep- check
Health and Nutrition-check
Exercise-check
Education-check
Relationships-check
Financial Intelligence-check
Work-check

Here it was, clear as day, or at least perfectly clear if your paying attention and looking at the whole thing logically.
Really, a clear pill? or, following a success system of habits to make transformational change, removing distractions and focusing on these habits to provide the drive and the life Eddie was eager to acquire.

Drive

"I'm not gifted, I'm driven." David Goggins

In this powerful statement by David Goggins, he rejects the notion of relying on innate gifts and highlights the significance of relentless determination. Goggins emphasises that his success isn't attributed to inherent talent but rather to an unyielding drive. It's a call to action, encouraging individuals to cultivate a tenacious work ethic and perseverance, ultimately transcending perceived limitations through sheer determination and effort.

On a personal note, I have always had a fire in my belly, in my younger days when I played football on a Sunday morning if we were 2-0 down with a minute on the clock I always thought we could score 3 goals and win the game, which must have made me a nightmare to play with when everyone else had conceded defeat.
Even now at 56 years of age I find myself on the treadmill surrounded by others or in the busy boxing room thinking to myself "this fellas leaving before me," as I dig in and keep going,, like an old git pushing his way to the front of the queue for his pension, my delusions of grandeur amuse me no end.

Being consistently driven though fuels my engine of progress, injecting purpose into my day, channelling my energy towards my goals and aspirations.
Being driven isn't merely about reaching the destination; it's about relishing the journey, savouring each step forward and living in and enjoying the now, without apology.
When you want to achieve something no matter what, it's your drive and the consistency of your actions that gets you there.

When everyone's going to Nando's I'm going NENDO- No Excuses No Days Off! This is the attitude I use as it helps me maintain focus.

Maintaining Focus

"Concentration comes out of a combination of confidence and hunger." - Arnold Palmer

Arnold Palmer, the legendary golfer, emphasised that concentration is not merely about focusing one's attention but stems from a potent blend of confidence and hunger.

Confidence provides the mental fortitude to believe in one's abilities, while hunger instills a relentless drive to achieve success. When these two elements intersect, concentration becomes a force that propels individuals toward their goals with unwavering determination and clarity of purpose.

When I was almost 19 stone in weight I decided that I was going to focus on running. In the past my attitude had always been "well I'm not a runner", thereby giving myself an excuse to fail before I'd even started, however with my reinvigorated attitude I asked myself a question. As I looked round the gym on the treadmills I spotted a few people I considered to be runners, you can tell them, the vest the check of the watch, the warm up, the focus in their eyes, and they're off like Mo Farah. "What have I got to do to be that? Not like that, not something like that, what exactly have I got to do to be a runner?" Answer, run, every day no matter what.

So I started, and after 5 minutes I was fighting for air like a granny trying to blow out trick candles on her 90th birthday.
I had decided however that I was going to stay on that treadmill for 1 hour no matter what so I walked the next 55 minutes. The next day I managed to run 7 minutes and walked for 53. The next day it was 10 minutes and a 50 minute walk.

I continued with these small marginal gains, every day adding to my time until something amazing happened, 35 minute run, 25 minute walk, I had reached the point where my run exceeded my walk

My success system for life had not taken a day off and I was beginning to see the positive results as I continued to be accountable for my actions.

Accountability

"Accountability is the glue that ties commitment to results." - Brian Tracy

Brian Tracy, a renowned motivational speaker, stresses the critical role of accountability in achieving tangible results. He argues that accountability serves as the binding force that transforms mere commitments into measurable outcomes. When individuals hold themselves or others accountable for their actions and decisions, they become more responsible and committed to fulfilling their goals. This accountability fosters a culture of reliability and follow-through, ultimately driving progress and success.

I had set my life up in my mind like a military operation.
Bed 9.00pm every night
Wake, no alarm 5.30am every morning
healthy breakfast every day
Work 6.00am-9.00am Monday-Saturday
Gym 9.15-11.30 every day
Shower and healthy lunch every day
Education/research/writing 12.30-3.30 everyday
Catch up with family and friends every day
reflect and progress plan for the next day, everyday
Healthy tea with family or friends everyday
relax and watch a movie to switch off
Bed 9.00pm day smashed, sleep

Holding myself accountable and responsible lead to massive personal growth.

My personal accountability cultivated the discipline I needed, driving consistent effort towards my goals. The positive feeling I had toward myself is like nothing I have ever experienced. Once I began to see the transformational change I knew I would never be the same, and for that I will be eternally grateful.

Gratitude

Gratitude can transform common days into thanksgivings, turn routine jobs into joy, and change ordinary opportunities into blessings." - William Arthur Ward

William Arthur Ward highlights gratitude's transformative potential, turning routine into joy and ordinary moments into blessings. Embracing gratitude infuses everyday life with thankfulness and appreciation, fostering fulfillment in simplicity. It empowers individuals to find joy in mundane tasks, recognising the abundance that surrounds them.

I find myself writing this and taking stock and I realise that one of the major elements responsible for supporting my transformational journey is my overwhelming feeling of gratitude towards every second I have been alive as I've learned so much about myself and realise I know basically nothing (which again brings a smile to my face) and I'm so grateful for my ignorance as it allows me to learn something new about myself everyday.

I am grateful that every morning, I get to work and see the sun rise, hear the birds sing, breath in the air of a new day, tend the gardens and make the place safe and adventurous for the little ones, drive to the gym, get my beast mode on and sweat for fun, engage and connect with amazing people, learn a million things from this great internet, get a front row seat to the crazy world we live in and smile and wonder how on earth we've made it this far.

The best thing for me personally though is waking from a deep sleep, no alarm and feeling that lovely jelly legs feeling and thinking, "the big fella hasn't called my number yet so let's get cracking stevie baby."

I keep an internal gratitude journal, noting daily blessings and positive experiences like laughing with loved ones.
I practice mindfulness, savouring the present moment and acknowledging simple joys like emptying my head as I run.
I express thanks regularly to loved ones, acknowledging their support and kindness, as I continue to grow in the art of being selfishly unselfish.

Selfishly Unselfish

"Friendship with oneself is all-important because without it one cannot be friends with anyone else in the world." -Eleanor Roosevelt.

Eleanor Roosevelt's quote underscores the pivotal role of self-care. By prioritising self-compassion and well-being, we cultivate meaningful relationships. It highlights that investing in personal growth is essential, not selfish, fostering deeper connections and enriching both personal and interpersonal experiences. Self-care is the foundation for genuine relationships and empathy.

I once thought that people who put themselves first were very selfish, and maybe some are, however I now have a different perspective. In order for me to give the best of myself I do need to put myself first otherwise how on earth am I able to give my best to anyone. When I began coaching boxing with a few lads at the gym I was almost 19 stone and I thought how am I supposed to advise anyone on fitness when I'm so unfit myself. Then when I thought about it further I asked myself an even greater question. What if I selfishly focus all my efforts on mastering the ultimate success system for life, and transform myself?
Will I then be better able to offer help to those looking to transform their lives?

I now believe being selfishly unselfish, paradoxically, enriches everyones life profoundly.
By prioritising self-care, unwavering responsibility and boundaries, this has enabled me to offer genuine help and support to others.

Chapter 5

Time

Time

"Time is the most valuable thing a man can spend." - Theophrastus

Theophrastus, an ancient philosopher, stresses time's utmost value, urging mindful spending. Each moment invested shapes life's trajectory, leaving an indelible mark. His wisdom highlights time's finite nature, emphasising thoughtful allocation for fulfillment. Thus, he prompts individuals to prioritise wisely, acknowledging its unparalleled significance in life's journey.

I'm often in the gym working out in the boxing area and end up chatting to people a lot younger than myself, where I make a point of asking their age, then go on to discuss their ambitions or if they are boxing just for fitness.
Some ask me and comment how I work hard and I thank them for their kindness, at 56 years of age I'm just in it for the fitness and I've always enjoyed punching the hell out of a bag as it has kept me sane over the years.

I explain that I train so hard because life is short and I understand one day it will be my last session, so I work hard and sweat and enjoy, as I am grateful for every single second and treat it as if it will be my last, because yesterday I was their age and today I'm 56.

When I say this most just smile, but there have been a few times where I can see by the expression on someone's face change, like I've touched something deep inside their soul and they understand exactly what I'm saying.

Or maybe they're just thinking, ""Stop talking shite you daft old git."

I have in my years come to understand that time is the most precious currency, an asset beyond measure and should be treated with the greatest care.
It really does feel that time speeds up as you get older and years pass so quickly as the pace of life refuses to slow down.

Today's 56 year-old self often yearns to counsel the 18-year-old version with some wise words;

"Treasure each heartbeat, seize opportunities, take calculated risks, relish every breath and live life to the fullest, but you're going to need a success system for your life because if you don't then life can become challenging and unknowingly hard when it needn't be".

Then, as I look upon my juvenile face, with teenager bad attitude and I hear the obligatory grunt, I would offer the following words of wisdom.

"And don't think because life's good at this moment and you think you know it all, that somewhere along the line a big huge boot won't fall out the sky and kick you right in the nuts out of nowhere, and try to break your soul because it will, and when it does you better be ready, and you better stick to your success system and get back up and kick back at life twice as hard, or it will bury you".

"Now what would you like for tea?.

I'm often asked by the young people I work with what I would do different if I had my time again.

It's an interesting question as I was leaving school just as mainstream technology was in its infancy and the world was very different, back in the day.

Nobody had a mobile phone, you had to find a telephone box (at the local shops usually, often vandalised and out of use) and put 10p in before you could even to speak to someone, and that was only if they were in.

The house phone was like the bat phone and could only be used on rare occasions and required express permission to use, in case someone rang, which it rarely did.

When it did ring everyone stopped what they were doing and time seemed to stand still as there was always an air of anticipation because you had no idea who it was until you answered.

Local Libraries and book stores were the hubs of information and if you wanted to learn anything you often had to trawl through 800 pages of a smelly tattered library book, in order to glean a selective piece of information as there was no google.

Television had a hand full of channels and you had to scan the tv guide or a newspaper to plan your viewing time and tune in, or you missed your programme and had no opportunity to catch up unless you were posh enough to have a video recorder. Now there's 1000 channels and everyone complains there's nothing on.

In order to meet a member of the opposite sex and arrange a date, you had to actually physically go up to someone and speak to them and ask them out, and often go through the embarrassment of rejection. There was no swiping right.

And if you were successful in getting a date you had to trust the other person to actually turn up as you didn't speak to them again, until the date. No 50 squillion messages back and forth.

If you wanted a takeaway meal you had to physically go to your preferred establishment and order and wait for your food and actually carry it home. Home delivery and Uber eats didn't exist. The thought of working from home would have been laughed at.

Yes the world was very different back in the olden days or as I fondly refer to them, the 1980's, where music was listened to mostly via a cassette tape or vinyl single or album, and the Sunday chart countdown on the portable radio was quite a big thing.

Hubba Bubba was the best chewing gum ever and pop stars were all the rage, and nobody ate at McDonald's.
Mars bars were huge and kids actually played out and took risks and some could be quite mischievous, but a hefty clip round the ear kept them in check if they went too far, no anti- social behaviour orders were necessary.
And for some reason throwing a stone at a lamp post from a distance and hitting it acted as permission to go home.

I often wonder where on earth did all that childhood fun go, and then I remember, the fun police took it away, or was it the advancement of technology.

It was a fantastic time though as I was leaving school and setting out to find my way in the world, without a clue, following the completion of my basic education.

In reflection would I do anything differently?
No, because every questionable decision and every mess up has been a fantastic learning experience and has led me to this point in what sometimes feels like 20 lives that I've lived?
If I was starting out today however, I'd have a field day.

Access to Information: Unparalleled access to knowledge and learning resources through the internet.
Global Connectivity: Easier networking and connections across the world, enabling opportunities beyond geographical limitations.
Entrepreneurial Opportunities: Platforms and tools for launching businesses and initiatives at a young age.

Technological Skills: Growing up in a tech-driven era fosters proficiency in digital skills from an early age.
Diversity and Inclusion: Increasing societal emphasis on diversity and inclusion can provide more opportunities for different backgrounds.
Flexibility in Career Paths: More flexibility to explore varied career paths and adapt to changing industries.

Those people who are switched on in todays world have the opportunity to succeed beyond measure, as all the information they require is at their fingertips, they just need to learn how to focus on their personal goals and navigate the many distractions that exist, once they find a way to leave the safety of their bedrooms and face the world head on.

I know, how about formulating a personal success system for life. Now there's a thought!

Chapter 6

Todays Challenges

Todays Challenges

There are a few crucial factors that require consideration however, because things aren't as clear as they first appear.

Information Overload: While there's plenty of information available, it can be overwhelming. Sorting through vast amounts of data to find credible, applicable knowledge can be challenging.

Lack of Direction: Having access to information doesn't necessarily equate to knowing how to apply it effectively. Without clear goals or direction, people might struggle to use information purposefully.

Execution Gap: Knowing what to do doesn't always translate to taking action and procrastination, fear of failure, or lack of motivation often hinder implementation.

Dependency on Technology: Ironically, excessive reliance on technology can lead to distractions, reducing productivity and focus on essential tasks.

Misinformation: Not all information available is accurate or beneficial and false or misleading data can misguide individuals, leading to wrong decisions or actions.

Lack of Soft Skills: Despite access to information, some individuals lack crucial soft skills like adaptability, communication, and problem-solving, which are essential for success in various domains.

To navigate these challenges and leverage technology and information effectively, one needs a blend of critical thinking, communication skills, goal setting, time management, adaptability, and a continuous learning mindset.

Success isn't solely about access to information but how that information is interpreted, applied, and integrated into one's life effectively.

I believe in order to fulfil ones greatest potential in today's world, following a system presents the greatest opportunity for success (of course I do, hence this book).

And the younger a person starts, the better.

The early foundational habits of sleep, health and nutrition, exercise, education and relationships should be skills that are developed from an early stage as soon as a young person can understand and adopt their benefits. Financial intelligence and work should also be introduced and experimented with in order to further prepare a young person for the transition into adulthood.

By cementing these habits into daily life, a young person may have a better idea as to what they may like to do when moving into adulthood, as they would already have an understanding of what a system of success is, and so would be better positioned to seek out a financial and work system that will offer the greatest chance of success in achieving their personal goals and ambitions.

Sounds pretty straight forward.

At 18 years old, an individual embracing a success system for life sets a strong foundation for an exciting and fruitful future.

Setting SMART (Specific, Measurable, Achievable, Relevant, Time-bound) goals across personal, academic, and career realms is pivotal.
Learning effective time and space management and organisational skills aids in prioritising tasks.

Continuous learning becomes crucial; seeking mentors, enrolling in relevant courses, and reading diverse material foster growth. Consistent implementation of The Magnificent Seven habits, fortifies physical and mental as well as social well-being in order for one to become a successfully, contributing member of society.

Financial literacy, investing, and saving habits from an early age pave the way for financial success.
Cultivating resilience, adaptability, and networking skills prepares for challenges and opportunities ahead.

Regular reassessment and adjustment ensure alignment with evolving ambitions.
Balancing short-term wins with long-term goals maintains motivation.

Embracing failures as learning experiences fosters resilience.

A support network of mentors, peers, and professionals serves as guidance and encouragement throughout the journey.

As a young person's life progresses, revisiting and revising goals, upgrading skills, and adapting to changes in the external environment would remain integral.
This lifelong commitment to personal growth, adaptability, and resilience would construct a robust success system propelling the young person through to the age of 65.

In today's world, there is immense pressure to succeed.
Fuelled by societal expectations, economic competitiveness, and the amplified portrayal of achievements on social media, individuals often experience immense pressure to excel.

This relentless pursuit of success can lead to stress, anxiety, and a distorted sense of self-worth.
Combatting the pressures to succeed involves fostering a culture of balance and self-compassion.

Encouraging realistic goals, promoting mental health awareness, and cultivating supportive communities or networks can help. Emphasising the value of personal well-being over relentless achievement aids in managing stress and restoring a healthier perspective on success.

Therefore adopting a personal success system for life becomes even more relevant and would help a young person to understand themselves a lot more.

Example

A personal success system for life from 18 to 65 years old.

Discovering life's direction as a young person often involves exploring interests, trying various activities, and gaining diverse experiences.

Reflecting on passions, values, and personal strengths, seeking mentorship, and being open to new opportunities can help clarify career or life aspirations over time.

18-25 years old:

Embed the foundational magnificent seven habits as a starting point on a life long prosperous journey of success and personal growth and understanding.

Education & Skill Development: Pursue higher education or vocational training aligned with passions and career goals.

Acquire soft skills like communication, problem-solving and leadership through internship, volunteering, or part- time jobs.

Financial Foundation:Learn budgeting, saving, and investing principles.
Start an emergency fund and explore low-risk investment options.

Networking & Mentorship:Engage with mentors or join professional networks relevant to career aspirations.

Build relationships and connections through social and professional gatherings.

For individuals aged 25 to 35, exploring career paths often involves building on past experiences, refining skills, and reassessing personal goals.

Networking, further education, seeking mentors, and pursuing varied experiences contribute to defining long-term career aspirations and life direction during this phase.

25-35 Years Old:

Personal success system for life: Embedded and being built on as life's opportunities, curve balls and obstacles begin to increasingly present themselves and require navigation.

Career Growth: Focus on career advancement, taking on challenging roles and seeking promotions.
Consider entrepreneurial ventures if inclined towards business ownership.

Financial Planning: Increase savings and investment contributions as income grows.
Explore diverse investment opportunities and consider real estate or passive income sources.

Personal Development: Prioritise work-life balance and self-care to avoid burnout.
Keep learning new skills to stay relevant in an evolving job market.

Between 35 and 50, individuals often focus on consolidating career achievements, possibly re-evaluating priorities, and seeking a balance between professional success and personal fulfilment.

This period might involve pursuing leadership roles, exploring entrepreneurial ventures, or seeking greater work-life harmony.

Reassessing goals and embracing growth opportunities become key.

35-50 Years Old:

Personal success system for life: Mastery of the magnificent seven or at least understanding fully and making adjustments to life if affected as ambitions and milestones in life are realised.

Wealth Accumulation: Maximise contributions to retirement accounts and investment portfolios.
Evaluate and adjust investment strategies to align with long-term financial goals.

Leadership & Contribution: Mentor younger professionals and engage in community or philanthropic activities.
Consider leadership roles or board positions in organizations aligned with values.

Health & Well-being become even more relevant as we age:
Continue to prioritise health with regular exercise and a balanced diet.
Invest in preventive healthcare and manage stress effectively.

Between 50 and 65, individuals may contemplate transitions, such as planning for retirement, exploring new interests or hobbies, or considering part-time work.

This phase often involves leveraging accumulated experience, potentially mentoring others, and finding avenues for personal fulfillment and contributions to society.

50-65+ Years Old:
Personal success system for life: Mastery and understanding of self and gratitude for a balanced and fulfilling life of wild and wonderful experiences.

Transition & Planning: Plan for retirement by assessing financial readiness and lifestyle choices.
Consider downsizing, relocating, or alternative retirement plans.

Legacy & Impact: Establish a will, estate plan, or charitable contributions for leaving a legacy.
Engage in activities that bring personal fulfilment and contribute positively to society.

Continued Learning & Adaptation: Stay updated with industry trends or explore new interests.
Embrace technology and adapt to changes in the economic landscape.

In order to achieve all of this some personal tools are going to be required as the roller coaster of life unfolds, and the more experiences we have the greater number of tools a person requires in order to navigate their personal, wonderful life.

Chapter 7

Emotional Elasticity

Emotional Elasticity

I want to touch on understanding something I describe as the emotional elastic band of life, as I believe it is of vital importance and contributes immensely towards the success system for life.

If someone has had a happy upbringing and things have generally gone their way, and they had love support and direction, then it may be fair to say their emotional elastic band may be stretchy at the good end but prone to snap at the bad end, due to limited experience of anything negative or bad happening in their life. (Most things good and bad happen to everyone at some point in life and it's just a matter of when, the example is for illustration and understanding purposes).

On the other hand if someone has faced hardship and trauma at an early age then it could be safe to say that their elastic band may be stretchy and full of calluses at the bad end due to the many times it has snapped and had to be tied back together, and as a result not so stretchy at the good end, due to the limited number of positive life experiences.

Also, coping with successes in life can bring its own problems, an example could be when someone wins the lottery and they have no idea how to handle a large amount of money as they may have always been poor and are unable to handle such a windfall, and blow it all in a short time.

Therefore the emotional elastic band mirrors feelings stretched to their limits before snapping or recoiling.
It symbolises resilience, capable of enduring stress but vulnerable to overextension. Initially pliable, it absorbs tension, yet with continuous strain, it risks reaching a breaking point.

Understanding this band signifies recognising the delicate balance between stretching oneself and safeguarding against an overwhelming burden.

It epitomises the need for self awareness, moderation and self care to prevent emotional strain from reaching its snapping point. The person with a traumatic childhood may develop a broader emotional elastic band if their life moving forward is mixed with positive experiences.

Their experiences can foster resilience, stretching their emotional capacity to endure adversity.
Having navigated hardships, they develop coping mechanisms, empathy, and adaptability, expanding their emotional range.

In contrast, someone raised in a happy, positive environment may possess a more limited band, having encountered fewer challenges.
While their foundation is stable, it might lack the flexibility needed to handle intense stressors.

The breadth of the emotional elastic band for those with traumatic pasts results from enduring and overcoming adversity, shaping them into resilient individuals.

The impact of a wider emotional elastic band from a traumatic childhood can manifest in various ways in adult life, and those it has affected should develop an understanding so they can navigate further challenges in a measured way.

Those who've experienced trauma might display heightened resilience, adaptability, and empathy, enabling them to handle stress more effectively.
However, they might also struggle with trust issues, emotional regulation, or experience triggers that revive past traumas, influencing relationships and decision-making.

Conversely, individuals from stable backgrounds might face challenges when confronting significant adversities as they move through life and might not possess the skills or coping mechanisms developed through overcoming past hardships.
Both paths can shape adult behaviours, influencing how individuals respond to stress, relationships, and the navigation of life's complexities.

On a personal note I think this is part of the reason I have been able to bounce back many times, as my emotional elasticity has been stretched and snapped and rebuilt many times over the years.

As a result I've always had the ability to shrug it off when life goes belly up and after a short period of lunacy, just dust myself down, give my head a shake and start again.
On the other hand, I can be over the top emotional when something really good has happened, and my gratitude bell goes off and it's like I've been gifted the holy grail when someone smiles and offers me a boiled sweet, because I feel that there is some kind of connection.

Chapter 8

It's All Connected

Its All Connected

As we move forward on this journey together, I want to impress on you a powerful truth: mastery is not a destination, it is a continuous process of growth, refinement, and evolution. This book is not just about a set of habits to check off a list; it is a way of life, a framework that integrates seamlessly into every decision, action, and goal you pursue.

You now have the knowledge, the structure, and the power to take control of your life. But knowledge without action is meaningless. The key to true transformation lies in consistently applying what you have learned, refining your habits, and striving for mastery in each of the seven foundational elements.

The question you must now ask yourself is this: What will I do with this knowledge?

Will you let it fade into the background, another book on the shelf, another idea that sounded good in theory but never became a reality?

Or will you take full ownership of your future and commit to integrating these principles into the very fabric of your life?

The choice is yours.

The Interconnected Nature of the Magnificent Seven
One of the most important lessons is the deep interconnectedness of these seven foundational habits. They do not exist in isolation. Each one affects and influences the others, creating a ripple effect that can either elevate or diminish your overall success and well-being.

When you strengthen one area, the benefits naturally extend into the others. But the opposite is also true—neglecting one can create a cascade of negative consequences. This is why true mastery requires balance and commitment across all seven areas.

Ok let's explore this balance wheel of success.

WHEEL OF SUCCESS

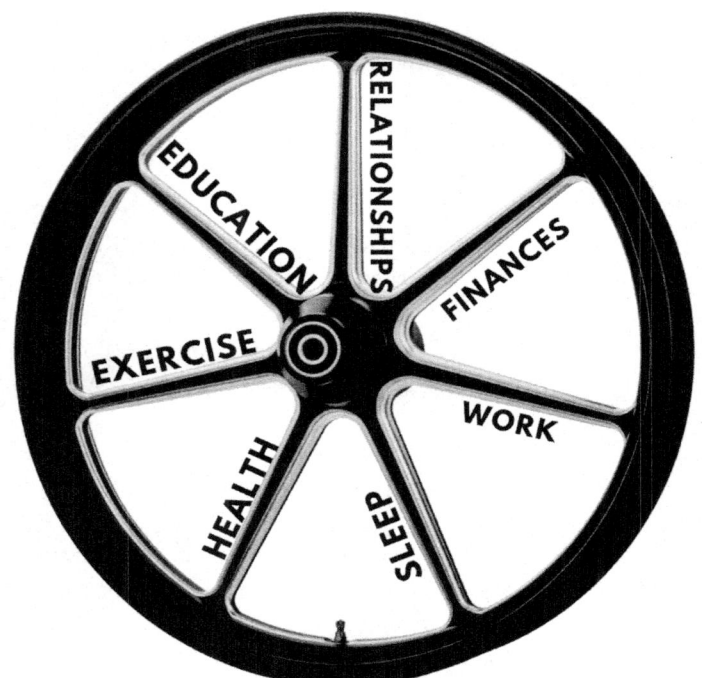

GLIDES AT SPEED

The Wheel as a Living System
Visualise a bicycle wheel and seven sturdy spokes. The hub is our sense of purpose; the rim is resilience—the strength that keeps the wheel from splintering under life's bumps. The spokes represent each one of The. Magnificent Seven habits: **sleep; health & nutrition; exercise; education (lifelong learning); relationships; financial intelligence; and work**. Remove any spoke and, at first, the wheel still turns, but each revolution warps it a little more until the rim collapses. In biological, psychological, and social terms the same domino-damage occurs inside us. Exploring each spoke in turn and then their interaction reveals why true well-being is never a single achievement but a synchronised system.

Spoke One – Sleep: Your Brain's Built-In Shock Absorber
Think of your life like a wheel, and sleep is the spoke that absorbs all the bumps along the road. When you get good, deep sleep, your brain actually goes into cleaning mode, flushing out waste and keeping your mind sharp and focused. But here's the twist: both too little and too much sleep can mess with your brain. When your sleep is off, the whole wheel starts to wobble. You feel foggy, moody, and suddenly those sugary snacks look really tempting, which puts extra pressure on your nutrition. The easiest way to start fixing it? Just go to bed and wake up at roughly the same time every day (within an hour's range). That simple habit helps reset your internal body clock and brings balance back to the system.

Spoke Two – Nutrition: The Fuel That Powers Everything
If sleep is the shock absorber, nutrition is the fuel line that keeps the engine running smoothly. Science is now showing us that nutrients like vitamin D, zinc, and omega-3s don't just help us feel better, they actually power up your immune system and fight off long-term inflammation, the sneaky kind that can wear down your heart and brain over time.

On the flip side, diets full of ultra-processed foods loaded with salt, sugar, and unhealthy fats clog up that fuel line. They cause low-level inflammation that makes you tired, foggy, and less able to focus. Even worse, bad eating habits can ruin your sleep and cancel out the benefits of exercise. The bottom line? You can't out-jog a junk food diet any more than you can fix a cracked bike wheel by pedaling harder. You've got to fuel the ride right from the start.

Spoke Three – Exercise: Turning Fuel into Forward Motion
Exercise is the spoke that gets the whole wheel spinning. It takes the good sleep and clean fuel from nutrition and turns it into momentum. A little movement every day beats the "weekend warrior" routine.

Exercise keeps your joints healthy, your blood sugar stable, and even helps your brain by releasing molecules that act like grease for your mental gears. But here's the kicker, when your workout routine suddenly crashes (you're tired, injured, or just can't be bothered), it's often a red flag that something deeper is off, like poor sleep or a bad diet. That's why smart exercise plans build in variety and rest days (for some), keeping all the spokes strong and the wheel rolling smoothly.

Spoke Four – Lifelong Learning: Your Built-In Balance Sensor
While other spokes keep the body in shape, learning keeps your mind balanced. It's like a gyroscope that senses when things are off and helps you correct course. And it's not just about reading books, learning new skills actually changes your brain's wiring. Learning also fires up the brain's reward system, the same one exercise triggers. That means it feels good and does good. But when learning stops due to stress, self-doubt, or just being stuck in the same routine your mental balance slips. People can fall into unhelpful habits, make bad financial decisions, or get stuck in relationships that don't work, all because they've stopped updating their thinking.

The fix doesn't have to be big: a 20-minute podcast, a quick online course, or even jotting down what you're curious about each day can reawaken that inner compass.

Spoke Five
Relationships: The Web That Holds Everything Together
If food is the fuel and exercise moves the wheel, relationships are the strong webbing that holds the whole thing together.
But this spoke isn't just about survival, it's about resilience. Being socially active helps you adapt to stress, keeps your emotions more balanced, and protects your mental health. On the flip side, when this spoke breaks say from isolation, a toxic relationship, or just drifting away from people, everything else starts to crack. Loneliness spikes stress hormones, messes with your sleep, fuels emotional eating, drains your bank account, and even tanks your job performance.

The fix? Don't treat friendship like a bonus, it's essential maintenance. Schedule regular hangouts, go for walks together, cook a meal, or just check in with someone once a week. These little habits don't just strengthen your relationships, they reinforce your entire life wheel.

Spoke Six – Financial Intelligence: The Stress Regulator
Money might not buy happiness, but mishandling it definitely buys stress. It's like grit in the wheel's bearings, no matter how well the other spokes are working, financial anxiety can grind everything down. Even people earning decent salaries aren't immune. If your debt is too high, sleep suffers, mood drops, and anxiety spikes. But there's good news: building financial intelligence, knowing how to budget, invest, save, and protect yourself with insurance, gives you back a sense of control.
Because money touches everything, from the cost of healthy food to gym memberships to continuing education, being financially unaware weakens all the other spokes. The good news? Just like with exercise, small, regular habits win the long game. A little budgeting today or a monthly investment adds up more than occasional financial windfalls.

Spoke Seven – Work: Where the Pressure Hits the Road

Work is the spoke where life's outside pressure meets your inner balance. Deadlines, shift schedules, meetings, they all put weight on the wheel, and how that load is carried can either strengthen you or wear you down. When work feels worthwhile, people stick around and thrive.

The best kinds of jobs give you three things that help your whole life run better:

- Competence (you are good at what you do)
- Autonomy (you have some control over how you do it)
- Connection (you feel like you're part of something that matters)

When work feels pointless or overwhelming, it's like a bent spoke warping the whole rim. Burnout creeps in. You skip workouts, grab fast food, and get snappy with the people you care about. The key question shifts from "How do I earn a paycheck?" to "How does my work help move me toward a life I value?" Because if that spoke stays misaligned too long, the whole wheel starts to wobble, and eventually, it just can't turn.

THE UNBALANCED WHEEL

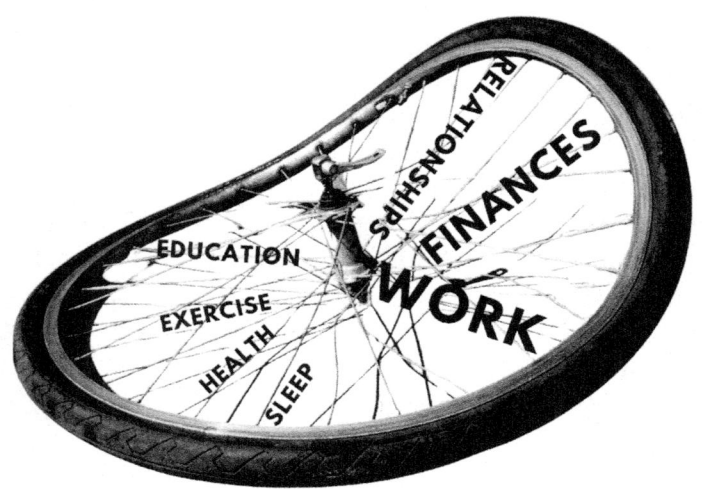

Example
Interdependence in Action: When One Spoke Breaks, the Whole Wheel Wobbles

Picture Jill, a 38-year-old graphic designer. A big project at work forces her onto late-night shifts, and suddenly she's only sleeping five hours a night. The first spoke sleep starts to crack.

Tired and foggy, she reaches for energy drinks and takeout (there goes nutrition). Too drained to hit the gym, she skips workouts (exercise falters). Her brain's too fried for her evening design class (learning slips), and she bails on weekend plans with friends (relationships suffer).

She forgets to pay a bill, racks up a late fee (finances wobble), and though she delivers the project, she feels empty and disconnected at work (purpose dims).

One small imbalance caused a total cascade.
But here's the empowering part: the fix works the same way. Start with just one spoke, like restoring regular, quality sleep.

That one shift gives her more energy. Better food choices come naturally. She's motivated to exercise again. Her mind clears, and she's back in her evening class. She reconnects with friends. Her money's back on track. Work starts to feel meaningful again.

This is why one-size-fits-all self-help advice so often falls flat. You can't just force one spoke tight while the others sag. The wheel still wobbles. True balance comes from systemic thinking. Everything is connected.

Conclusion: From Struggle to Flow Turning Momentum Into Mastery

When your wheel is well-balanced, something magical happens: a gentle push carries you far. Life flows. Progress feels natural.

Each spoke supports the others:
Ignore one, and stress starts to spread like a crack in the rim. But nurture them together? Suddenly, you're not just coping, you're cruising.

So next time life feels off-track, don't panic. Just pause and ask: Which spoke feels loose right now?
Tighten that one gently. Then check the others. That's the secret, not perfection, but synergy.

And once your wheel is balanced you can apply more energy to your life.

Energy

When I was fat I always felt like I had little to no energy. I was tired all the time and my mood swings were often more than a cause for concern.

Part of me knew it was my attitude and my mindset, and I was great at making my age an excuse. Once I began my transformational journey and began to apply The Magnificent Seven, I began to look at energy in a different way.

Sleep became a priority and a 9.00pm bed time routine became the first action I took that reset my body and I began to wake naturally without an alarm at around 5.00am with a clear head and boundless energy. The new healthy eating plan also had a major affect as I was going to bed on an empty stomach and the food I was now consuming was for fuel not gluttonous satisfaction.

At the gym I was able to put more energy into my workouts which meant I was beginning to feel fantastic, and my weight was coming down so I could see the difference it was making. I was excited about learning as my research on the Seven increased as I fine tuned my system.

My relationships were now all positive and for the first time in my life I wasn't listening to people gossiping and energy draining drama. Financially I was in a much stronger position and was amazed at how little I needed to live on once I introduced my system (I also had a lot of help in this area).

My work was all encompassing now as my gratitude attitude was in full force as my service to others mindset gave me an extra energy boost.

The Flow State

As my research continued I looked into burnout and flow as I wanted to be as informed as possible, due to the fact I was "getting on a bit".

One day I was on the treadmill running (this was after the weight loss and the disappearance of the grandad shuffle) when I entered a state I can only describe as complete focus as I lost all concept of time and my run became effortless as I imagined myself travelling through endless space. My breathing was noticeably easy as If I wasn't breathing air but I was tapped into some whole other energy field.

I remember feeling the same experience many years ago when I was taking part in the Great North Run and it was as if the energy flowing through me was coming from the other runners around me. It was an unusual experience and somewhat euphoric which is why I recalled it.

Following some research into the subject of quantum energy flow I realised that I had created the magnificent seven as a system of flow where everything is in balance and instead of pushing and trying harder to speed things up and get there quicker (as I had done most of my life), I had actually relaxed and let go and suddenly the energy I had thought I was generating was instead flowing through me effortlessly.

It was this shift from effort to alignment that revealed something deeper, that what we perceive to be our own force or struggle might actually be a resonance with something greater. And what made the difference wasn't the circumstances or the event itself, but my perspective.

We often think of perception as passive, the eyes seeing, the ears hearing, the body feeling. But perception is more than sensing; it's the lens through which we interpret experience. One person might feel drained running among a crowd, while another is uplifted by the collective energy. The event is the same, but the internal framing or the perspective, transforms the experience entirely.

That moment during the run, and later during my work with the Magnificent Seven, taught me that energy, flow, and even success are deeply tied to how we choose to see our world.

When our perspective shifts from resistance to receptive, from isolation to interconnection, perception itself changes. We begin to notice things we'd overlooked, to feel energies we once blocked out, to trust in movement instead of control.

Chapter 9

Perception vs Perspective

Perception Vs Perspective
It is crucial to differentiate perception from perspective.

- Perception is the way we interpret sensory input and information. It is often immediate, emotional, and shaped by biases, past experiences, and current mental states. Perception is subjective and sometimes distorted, as it is based on limited data.
- Perspective, on the other hand, is a broader, more reflective understanding of a situation. It involves stepping back, seeing the bigger picture, considering context, long-term consequences, and other viewpoints beyond our immediate feelings. Perspective is more balanced and less reactive.

When applied to The Magnificent Seven, perception can lead to narrow or impulsive judgments, while perspective allows for wise decisions and sustainable balance. For example, someone might perceive exercise as exhausting and time-consuming (a negative lens) but, with perspective, they would see it as an investment in long-term health and energy.

Let's explore how perception and perspective influence each of the seven habits positively and negatively and why perspective provides a more balanced, empowering way to approach life.

Sleep: Rest or Waste of Time?

Perception (Positive):
Some people see sleep as a well-earned treat—a time to unwind, recharge, and take care of themselves. They enjoy the calm, the comfort, and the feeling of waking up refreshed.

Perception (Negative):
Others see sleep as dead time—hours they could be spending hustling, socialising, or binge-watching something "more productive." In our go-go-go culture, sleep is often treated like an obstacle instead of a necessity. The result? Chronic exhaustion that creeps into every part of life.

Perspective:
Step back, and the picture changes completely. Sleep isn't a break from progress—it's what makes progress possible. It clears your mind so you can learn, restores your body so you can move, steadies your emotions so you can connect, and fuels your focus for meaningful work. Seen through the right lens, sleep isn't optional—it's your power source. The real waste? Running on empty.

Nutrition: Restriction or Fuel for Life?

Perception (Positive):
Some people look at healthy eating as an act of self-love. They enjoy the vibrant colors, fresh flavors, and the pride that comes from taking care of their bodies. They see food as nourishment, not just for the body, but the mind and soul.

Perception (Negative):
Others see it as a buzzkill. "Healthy" equals bland, expensive, or inconvenient. Why eat salad when chips are faster and tastier? In the short term, taste and time win out, while long-term health takes a backseat.

Perspective:
But zoom out, and nutrition becomes more than a meal, it becomes momentum. The right food sharpens your thinking, stabilises your mood, improves sleep, and powers your workouts. It reduces your risk of disease and even affects how well you handle stress or show up in relationships. From this viewpoint, eating well isn't about restriction, it's a strategy. One that energises every other part of your life.

Exercise: Pain or Personal Power?

Perception (Positive):
For some, exercise is a feel-good ritual. It boosts energy, lifts mood, and builds confidence. They see it as a source of strength, not just physically, but mentally and emotionally.

Perception (Negative):
Others see exercise as a chore. It feels painful, exhausting, or something only "fit people" do. With this mindset, working out becomes an obligation rather than an opportunity, leading to skipped sessions and guilt-driven starts and stops.

Perspective:
Zooming out, exercise becomes something far more meaningful. It's not just about looks or discipline, it's about freedom. The freedom to move through life with strength and confidence. Exercise supports better sleep, lowers stress, sharpens thinking, and boosts resilience in the face of work or personal challenges. Seen through this lens, movement isn't punishment, it's self-maintenance. It's how you keep the wheel rolling strong.

Education: Obligation or Ongoing Growth?

Perception (Positive):
Some people see learning, whether it's a podcast, book, or new skill as a chance to grow. It excites them. They view education as self-improvement, not a requirement.

Perception (Negative):
Others see it as a drag. "School's over," or "I don't have time." Learning feels hard, boring, or only necessary if you're after a diploma or promotion.

Perspective:
With the right perspective, education becomes much more than homework. It's your lifelong upgrade system. Every new thing you learn sharpens your mind, helps you solve problems better, improves communication, builds empathy, and deepens financial and career decisions. Education isn't just something you finish—it's something that finishes you, shaping who you are becoming in every season of life.

Relationships: Obligation or Lifeline?

Perception (Positive):
When viewed positively, relationships are a source of warmth, support, and joy. People with this mindset see time spent with loved ones as meaningful, something that adds depth and richness to life.

Perception (Negative):
Others see relationships as complicated or draining. They might avoid closeness to dodge emotional discomfort or see social time as a distraction from their personal goals. In this view, connection becomes optional or worse, a burden.

Perspective:
But from a wider perspective, relationships aren't just nice to have, they're essential. Strong social bonds reduce stress, improve emotional health, and make life's challenges easier to bear. Relationships are the thread that weaves everything else together. Achievements in work, money, or learning mean more when they're shared. From this lens, relationships aren't obligations, they're investments that multiply life's rewards.

Financial Intelligence: Stress or Strength?

Perception (Positive):
For some, managing money feels empowering. It offers freedom, peace of mind, and the ability to make choices, whether that's taking a trip, changing careers, or helping someone in need.

Perception (Negative):
For others, money feels overwhelming or irrelevant. Budgeting seems restrictive, investing feels confusing, and some adopt the belief that "money isn't everything," using that as a reason to avoid learning how to manage it.

Perspective:
Step back, and you'll see money not as a source of stress, but as a support system. Financial intelligence isn't about greed or perfection; it's about using resources wisely to improve your quality of life. It affects your sleep, nutrition, education, relationships, and even career choices. With the right perspective, managing money becomes a form of self-care, and a gateway to freedom, not restriction.

Work: Duty or Purpose?

Perception (Positive):
When people see work in a positive light, they view it as a meaningful way to contribute, grow, and accomplish something bigger than themselves. It gives them a sense of pride and direction.

Perception (Negative):
Others see work as a grind or just something to survive. It feels draining, repetitive, and disconnected from who they are. This often leads to burnout, resentment, or checking out emotionally.

Perspective:
With a shift in perspective, work becomes just one spoke in the larger wheel of life. It's a tool not your entire identity. Yes, work can provide purpose and progress, but it shouldn't come at the cost of your health, relationships, or joy. Perspective helps you ask the bigger question: "Is this work helping me build a life I value?" When work is aligned with your values and balanced with the other spokes, it becomes energising instead of exhausting.

The Interconnectedness of Perception and Perspective

Let's say you perceive work as nothing but duty. You stay late, skip workouts, sleep less, and cancel plans with friends. That one perception slowly pulls the rest of your wheel out of balance.
But here's the good news: perspective works the same way, only in reverse.
Reframing sleep as a non-negotiable part of performance boosts your energy, mood, and focus.
Viewing exercise as empowerment builds confidence that spreads into how you handle challenges.

Seeing financial intelligence as freedom reduces stress and opens space for deeper relationships and clearer goals.

Perspective creates a positive ripple effect. It connects the dots, strengthens your wheel, and helps you move through life with more flow and less friction.

Why Perspective Beats Perception Every Time

Perception is reactive. Perspective is wise.
Perception is what we feel in the moment. It's short-term, emotional, and often shaped by stress, mood, or habits

Perspective, on the other hand, zooms out. It sees beyond today. It asks, "How will this choice affect me tomorrow, next week, or five years from now?"

Take sleep, for example.
Perception says: "I need to stay up and finish this project, it's productive."

Perspective says: "Without rest, my focus, mood, and health will suffer, and so will the quality of my work."

One is driven by urgency; the other by wisdom.

Perspective Sees the Bigger Picture
- Perception is narrow and personal. It's often clouded by stress or bias.
- Perspective integrates your values, goals, and relationships. It helps you step outside the moment and ask, "What really matters here?"

When you're caught in a tough decision or feeling overwhelmed, perspective is the voice that brings calm and clarity. It reminds you that your habits don't exist in isolation, they work as a team.

Perspective Builds Resilience
Challenges are inevitable, money problems, work pressure, relationship hiccups.
Perception can make them feel like the end of the world.
Perspective reminds you: "I've been here before. I've got tools. This moment will pass."
It keeps you steady when life gets bumpy.

Perspective Creates Balance
Life gets unbalanced when one area takes over, like when work crowds out sleep, movement, or connection. Perception may say, "This is urgent, just focus on this."

Perspective asks, "At what cost?"

It helps you keep all the spokes of your life wheel in check, so the ride stays smooth.

The Real Benefits of Living with Perspective

When you look at your habits through the lens of perspective, everything shifts. Here's what you gain:

- Clarity & Focus – You stop guessing which part of your life needs attention. You know.
- Lower Stress – You accept that balance is fluid, not perfect, and that's okay.
- Empowerment – You stop seeing habits as chores and start seeing them as fuel for the life you want.
- Consistency – Small, intentional steps beat emotional swings and burnout every time.
- Holistic Growth – Your habits stop competing and start working together. The wheel spins smoother, stronger, farther.

Final thought:
Perception reacts.
Perspective responds.
When you live from a place of perspective, you stop chasing balance, and start building it…….. like a pyramid (of sorts).

Chapter 10

Pyramid of Success

The Magnificent Seven as a Pyramid of Success

Picture personal growth as a seven-layer pyramid. Its wide foundation is made of the basics that keep a human organism alive and learning, sleep, health and nutrition, physical exercise; education (formal and informal), relationships, financial intelligence, work. In childhood and early adulthood the base layers (sleep, health and nutrition, exercise, education, relationships) are naturally wide: parents enforce bedtimes, schools require continual learning, play keeps bodies moving, and friendships spring up effortlessly. At the narrow summit sits "work" because, at first, society gives young people relatively little of it.

Somewhere between the end of school and mid-career, however, many people flip that pyramid on its head. Work and money occupy most hours, while the so-called "foundation" layers become thin, optional edges.

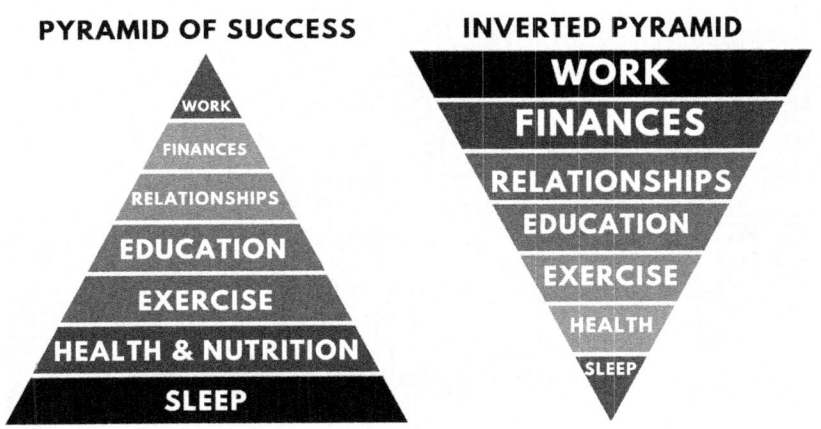

By the time many people reach retirement, something subtle but significant has happened. What was once a solid foundation of rest, energy, movement, curiosity and connection, a has often been flipped on its head.
Instead of being supported by healthy habits, fulfilling relationships, and a sense of purpose, life is now precariously balanced on a base of decades of overwork, too little sleep, inconsistent exercise, meals eaten in a rush, frayed social ties and a long-forgotten sense of wonder.

Sound familiar?

This inversion isn't just a personal issue. It contributes to widespread chronic disease, mental burnout, and loneliness, burdens that ripple through families, workplaces, healthcare systems, and entire economies.

The Pyramid of Personal Growth

Level	Habit	Rationale for its position
1	Sleep	The only behaviour without which humans die in days. Governs cognitive performance, immunity, emotional regulation.
2	Health & Nutrition	Food, hydration, preventive healthcare—fuel and maintenance of the organism.
3	Exercise	Mechanically stresses muscles, bones, and the cardiovascular system to keep them functional; also a major antidepressant.
4	Education	Builds cognitive maps, adaptability, and self-efficacy.
5	Relationships	Social mammals need belonging; relationships buffer stress and extend longevity.
6	Financial Intelligence	Competence with money enables autonomy and risk management without becoming life's sole purpose.
7	Work	A vehicle for purpose, contribution, and income—valuable, but resting on the health, skills, and relationships beneath it.

Life-Course Dynamics and the Drift Toward Inversion

Early life: A naturally upright pyramid
Children have guardians who schedule meals and sleep, teachers who enforce education, sports embedded in play, and friends assigned by classroom proximity. Work and money hardly register. In other words, societal scaffolding keeps the pyramid upright even when the child has no theory of pyramids at all.

Emerging adulthood: Autonomy without wisdom
University or first jobs hand young adults control over bedtimes, diet, exercise, budgeting, friendship maintenance, and work hours, often before habits are crystallised. Cognitive psychologists call this a self-regulation gap: the prefrontal cortex is still maturing while external rules loosen. Partying until 3 a.m. before an 8 a.m. lecture feels survivable, so sleep shrinks first. Cheap fast food replaces home cooking. The pyramid tilts.

Career building and family formation
By the late twenties and thirties two forces collide:
1. Labour-market competition rewards over-investment in work hours (the "greedy jobs" problem).
2. Family formation adds childcare and mortgage payments, elevating financial intelligence from academic interest to perceived life-or-death necessity.

Time becomes the zero-sum currency. Sleep, exercise, and friendships are robbed to pay the mortgage and impress the boss. Because health effects are delayed, the cost feels abstract.

Mid-career to pre-retirement
Promotions bring higher income but also expectation escalation: bigger houses, private schooling, status consumption. Economists label this the hedonic treadmill. Simultaneously, biological resilience falls, metabolism slows, body clock rhythms shift, joints wear. Yet because identity is now entwined with professional role, people respond not by right-sizing work but by doubling down. The pyramid is effectively upside-down.

Late career and retirement
The abrupt removal of work (retirement) unmasks the neglected base layers. Relationships fade or disappear if they were tied mostly to the workplace. Chronic diseases manifest. Brain plasticity drops. Financial anxiety can intensify because high spending habits outlive salary. Society now shoulders medical and caregiving costs.

Why Does the Inversion Happen? Seven Interlocking Forces
Delayed feedback loops:
Health inputs (diet, sleep) yield benefits or harms years later, whereas work outputs (salary, praise) arrive on the next paycheque. Humans, being present-biased, chase immediate reinforcement.

Social signalling and status economies:
In many cultures long hours and high income are status cues. Nobody brags about eight hours of unbroken sleep. The smartphone makes professional availability a public display (green dot = important person) while hiding quiet habits like cooking vegetables.

Economic insecurity and policy environment:
In countries without universal healthcare or affordable education, households self-insure by hoarding money. Employers often link health insurance to full-time work, perversely incentivising more hours to secure health benefits at the cost of health.

Technological acceleration:
Knowledge workers can extend their reach 24/7 via laptops and phones. Gig-economy platforms algorithmically encourage "just one more ride." Work expands to fill every temporal crevice (Parkinson's Law 2.0).

Urban design:
Suburban sprawl separates homes from workplaces and groceries; commuting erodes exercise time and encourages drive-through meals. Meanwhile modern housing isolates nuclear families, thinning neighbourly relationships.

Educational narratives:
Schooling often frames success as culminating in a prestigious job, not a balanced life. Financial literacy is taught (if at all) without equal emphasis on sleep hygiene or relational skills, reinforcing the idea that money outranks the other six habits.

Cognitive dissonance and sunk-cost fallacy:
Having invested decades in degrees and careers, people justify further sacrifices to "make it worthwhile," even if evidence suggests the trade-off is harming them. The more one's identity is "high achiever," the harder it is to exit the hamster wheel

Consequences of an Inverted Pyramid

Individual Health Outcomes
- Sleep debt raises risks of obesity, type 2 diabetes, cardiovascular disease, depression, and neurodegeneration (e.g., Alzheimer's).
- Poor nutrition plus sedentarism increases metabolic syndrome, some cancers, and musculoskeletal pain.
- Social isolation correlates with higher mortality than obesity or heavy smoking.
- Cognitive stagnation in later life accelerates memory decline

Psychological Costs
Burnout, anxiety, and "success emptiness" emerge when extrinsic goals (money, title) crowd out intrinsic ones. Even high incomes stop improving subjective well-being beyond moderate thresholds once basic needs and modest comforts are met.

Familial and Community Spill-overs
Parental overwork predicts lower child academic performance and mental health. Elder care often falls on daughters who reduce their own labour-force participation, perpetuating gender inequity. Communities lose volunteers, mentors, and civic leaders when citizens are time-poor.

Macroeconomic and Societal Costs
- Healthcare expenditure: chronic, lifestyle-related diseases account for the majority of spending in developed nations.
- Productivity losses: presenteeism (working while sick) costs more than absenteeism.
- Inequality: those with higher "well-being capital" (good health, strong networks) weather shocks better, widening gaps.
- Demographic pressure: unhealthy ageing populations shrink workforces and strain pensions.

Rebuilding Your Life from the Ground Up
How to Put Your Magnificent Seven Habits Into Practice

When life starts to feel out of balance, too much stress, too little energy, and not enough time for what really matters, it's often because the foundation is shaky. Over the years, it's easy to flip life upside down: work takes over, rest becomes a luxury, and the things that make you feel alive get pushed aside.
But there's a way back, and it starts by rebuilding your life from the base up using your Magnificent Seven Habits. These are the seven core areas that support lasting well-being and fulfillment:

Step 1: See Where Your Time Really Goes

Take one week (168 hours) and track how you spend your time. Color-code or label each hour based on the seven habits.
You might notice, for example, that "Work" gets 50+ hours… but "Sleep" barely gets 30, and "Relationships" don't even show up. This exercise helps you face the truth of where your energy is going, and where it's missing.

Step 2: Implementing The Magnificent Seven

You don't have to fix everything at once. Some habits naturally create a domino effect. For example:
- Getting better Sleep often improves your mood, your decision-making, and even your metabolism.
- Regular Exercise makes it easier to sleep, improves confidence, and lifts brain fog, which helps with work and learning.

Pick ONE habit from the Magnificent Seven to focus on first, and build consistency. Let it lift the others over time.

Step 3: Redefine What "Enough" Means
Financial Intelligence isn't just about earning more, it's knowing what's enough for you.

Try this:
- Define your "sufficient lifestyle", what really matters to you?
- Then ask: Are the extra hours you spend working worth the cost (missed meals, stress, time with loved ones)?

Knowing the trade-offs helps you work smarter, not just harder.

Step 4: Make Habits Social and Visible
We stick with habits more easily when we do them with others. Consider:
- A weekly walk + talk with a friend (Exercise + Relationships)
- A shared meal plan with your family (Health & Nutrition)
- A monthly money check-in with a partner or accountability buddy (Financial Intelligence)
- A learning group or book club (Education + Relationships)

Put these habits into your calendar and treat them like appointments.

Step 5: Check Your Direction
Every few years, pause and reflect:

If someone gave your eulogy tomorrow, what would they say about you?
Would they talk about your job title... or your kindness, your love of learning, your presence with your kids, your resilience?
Use this to re-align your time with what truly matters and shift focus back to the magnificent seven.

Rebalancing Starts With You
The Magnificent Seven aren't just a list, they're a map to a healthier, more meaningful life. But they work best when you actively build your day, your choices, and your energy around them.

Chapter 11

Deeper Thoughts

Deeper Thoughts

Now you have your Magnificent Seven habits clearly set out we can move on with a few old age thoughts that I hope you may find useful as an addition to your success system.

Some years back I recall attempting to teach my daughter how to ride her bike.
She was at the stage where she was good and confident with stabilisers on, but now came the time to take them off.
My word, she was like Bambi on ice! not a pretty site but quite funny at the same time, well funny for dad anyway.

Bless her she couldn't go two yards without falling over, despite me giving her a gentle balancing push from the back, which is how I learned.
We tried for hours and she kept saying " I can't do it!"
I had to admit I was at a bit of a loss because with the stabilisers on she was a cycling demon. (Deluded parent).

Then I thought "I know, I'll YouTube it!"
I click on to a video and this guy was advising to take the stabilisers off, and also the pedals and drop the seat so the child can reach the floor with their feet.
I remember thinking "No way, it can't be that simple!"
So we tried it and hey presto she was off.

The gist of it was, she was learning the foundational parts, to balance and steer, which meant she was focusing on controlling her hands and the direction and speed of the bike, whilst using her feet as the stabilising factor as she could reach the floor, which prevented her from falling.
She mastered this in five minutes.
So we put the pedals back on and that was it, a cyclist was born, as everything clicked in and off she pedalled.
The joy on her face had me in tears, I'm soft like that.

The point of the story is this.

You now have your foundational habits in place, which is like riding the bike without the pedals.

Now you have learned how to balance The Magnificent Seven and navigate the pitfalls.
We now need to put your pedals on so you can get to your destination, maybe learn how to pull a wheelie or an endo, or ride fast and skid to a stop while spinning the bike and looking impressive and feeling good about yourself.

We will treat the pedals as your dream goals and ambitions in life, as these are what give you the skills you need learn to improve on the basics and practice and master, in order to set you apart from others and lead you to your preferred destination, and the top of your personal podium.

I use this metaphor as I think it can illustrate how in life sometimes we lose focus of the foundational principles that have kept us steady and served us well.

Mainly in an attempt to reach our destination goals by focusing on what we think may look impressive to others, only for the wheels to come off at some point by failing to regularly reflect and ensure our positive habits are in place and in balance.

In this example we fail to regularly service the bike or become reckless, or reflect on our position to see where we are at in life and how we managed to get there and the lessons we learn along the way, and more importantly the person we have become.

Another thing. One has to be careful when embarking on a quest for personal success, as not everyone you know will be on board.

Dream Stealers and Naysayers

How many times have you had a business idea or wanted to tackle some challenge like a marathon and everyone you speak to has some comment as to why you shouldn't pursue your idea. "That sounds risky" or "such and such tried that and failed" or "there are loads of people doing that already, just come for a pint."
Every man and his dog will pee on your chips if you let them.

We have all heard this kind of negativity, often unfortunately from the people closest to us.

Dealing with naysayers and dream stealers requires resilience and focus. You must first recognise their negativity as a reflection of their own insecurities.

One way to overcome the dream stealers is to stay committed to your success system habits and your goals, understanding that not everyone will share your vision, and the best thing to do is not tell people and just do it.

Also it may be a good idea to learn to surround yourself with supportive individuals who uplift and inspire you, as well as challenge you to become greater.
Channel your energy into working on and improving yourself by maintaining a positive mindset.

Some say silence the doubters and prove them wrong.

I say "F**k them, and the horse they rode in on!"

Legacy Planning

My goal when setting out on my transformational road following the Pandemic and the lockdowns was to lose 3 stone and find some purpose and gratitude in the life that remained.
As a 54 year old man at the time who had lost everything including my sanity, and the will to live, this appeared to be quite an interesting challenge.

I was working on another project about the stages of life when I came to the section on legacy planning.
I found myself staring at the screen thinking of something to write. I thought of what people may say about me at my funeral "his farts we're really loud", "he used the word f**k a lot", "he had a canny sense of humour", " he never left me a bean".
I discovered however, that legacy planning involves a lot more than material possessions (fortunately). It's also about sharing life stories, experiences, and the wisdom one may gain throughout life..

I had always been one to value useful education, especially in relation to the realities of life, to ensure that knowledge and skills for whatever they were worth, were passed on to whoever was willing to listen which is fewer people than we think, as the old saying goes "nobody cares."
I had emphasised mostly to myself the importance of positive relationships and connections and even wrote a heartfelt letter expressing my love, hopes, and guidance, all the while wanting to preserve my memory in a meaningful way when I was gone.

This is what set me on the exciting adventure to research and create The Ultimate Success System For Life.
One year later and three stone lighter, surrounded by fantastic supportive people, my success system solid, I sleep and wake without an alarm, I attend the gym every day, my diet is cleaner than ever, although I do allow myself the odd treat.

Your Legacy

In order to transform into your best self, know you are armed with this information as your personal success system..
Be consistent and set yourself clear, realistic goals.
Prioritise your objectives and break them into manageable tasks and look for marginal gains over time rather than large quick wins that may lead to burnout and loss of interest.

Embrace drive, focus and adaptability, adjusting your strategies when needed.
Maintain a growth mindset, viewing challenges as opportunities for learning.
Cultivate consistency and discipline, as your daily habits will shape your long-term success.
Surround yourself with positive influences and seek mentorship.
Regularly assess your progress and celebrate small victories.
Nourish your mental and physical well-being through self-care.

Stay aligned with your core values and aspirations. by regularly refining your personal success system, embrace continuous improvement, and you can steadily evolve into your most empowered and fulfilled self.
Exude gratitude and humility and remember that you are in control and are responsible for the position you are in and that external factors that may present themselves as barriers only act as interesting obstacles to present exciting challenges that you must face and use your skills to overcome in order to grow.

Remember, a man with a plan is hard to beat, but a competent and capable man following a system, who has put the required number of hours in necessary to achieve that plan is virtually unstoppable.

Hopefully by now this has got you thinking, critically.

Critical Thinking

"Critical thinking is the key to unlocking the doors of understanding, enabling us to navigate the complexities of life with wisdom and discernment." - Albert Einstein

Critical thinking is a cognitive process that goes beyond mere acceptance of information. It involves actively analyzing, evaluating, and synthesizing information to form well-reasoned conclusions. In the journey of critical thinking, individuals cultivate the skill to question assumptions, consider alternative perspectives, and weigh evidence.

This intellectual discipline will empower you to navigate the intricacies of decision-making, problem-solving, and understanding the world around you. It's a continuous process of refining your thoughts, fostering intellectual curiosity, and embracing the complexity inherent in your pursuit of knowledge.

Applying critical thinking to The Ultimate Success System For Life.

When life feels like a maze, breaking down your path will help. if you Imagine your journey is the system, analysing the key components. Reflect on what really matters to you and seek stability beyond quick wins. Consider if your route aligns with fairness and lasting value. Life's twists need a resilient system.

Real stories can guide you and help you learn from them. It's about rediscovering your balance, not just for today but for a fulfilling tomorrow. You're not alone; many find their way by critically looking at where they've been. This helps In order to build a sustainable map that aligns with your values and leads to thinking big and creating lasting success.

Thinking Big

"The question is not what is your idea; the question is how big can you think" is often attributed to the renowned business and personal development author, Robert H. Schuller.

Schuller was a prominent motivational speaker and the founder of the Crystal Cathedral in California.
The quote underscores the significance of expansive thinking. Schuller, a prolific author and motivational speaker, urged individuals to transcend conventional limits in conceptualising ideas.

It encourages a mindset that stretches beyond immediate challenges, prompting one to envision possibilities on a grand scale.
By emphasising the size of one's thinking over the specific content of an idea, Schuller championed innovation and the pursuit of audacious goals.

This sentiment resonates in the entrepreneurial and self-help realms, urging individuals to dream boldly and foster a mentality that paves the way for extraordinary achievement's.

So, do you want to open a burger bar? Or, do you want to be McDonalds
A burger bar offers more customisation and artisanal options, appealing to niche markets and food enthusiasts. On the other hand, McDonald's provides a globally recognised brand with established systems and processes, catering to a broader audience seeking consistency and convenience. Plus they aren't in the burger business, they are in the real estate business, and the battle cry is "Im lovin it".

Discover Your Battle Cry

My wish is that you are now thinking big and have began your transformative process.
Embrace the wisdom of "how big can you think?" as a catalyst for your journey. Let Robert H. Schuller's words fuel a seismic shift in your perspective.

Break free from the constraints of ordinary thinking and dare to dream expansively.
Envision your most audacious goals and let them ignite your passion, using this mantra as a beacon, guiding you towards a future where your aspirations know no bounds.

The world craves your unique contribution. Seize the opportunity to craft a legacy defined by the magnitude of your dreams.
In the pursuit of greatness, remember that it begins with the enormity of your thoughts, and it flourishes through your unwavering commitment to turn those thoughts into reality.

As Admiral David Farragut during the American Civil War uttered, during the Battle of Mobile Bay in 1864:

"Damn the torpedoes, full steam ahead!"

Farragut's determination to press forward despite the danger has since become an enduring expression of courage and resolve in the face of adversity.

So forge ahead with your heart ablaze, your destiny awaits and the world is your oyster so communicate it effectively.

Effective Communication

"Communication is the bridge between confusion and clarity. Mastering it is the key to connecting hearts and minds, unlocking the doors to understanding and collaboration." - Oprah Winfrey.

Effective communication serves as the essential conduit that spans the gap between confusion and clarity. It goes beyond mere words, incorporating empathy and active listening to forge genuine connections In human interaction. Mastery of communication becomes the key that unlocks doors to shared understanding and collaboration.

Whether in personal relationships or professional endeavors, the art of communication is a powerful force, shaping the narrative of our interactions and fostering a harmonious exchange of ideas. It's a skill that transcends linguistic proficiency, embracing the nuanced dance of expression and reception, ultimately enriching the fabric of human connection.

In a job interview for example, effective communication extends beyond reciting your resume. It involves understanding the company's needs, actively engaging with interviewers, and tailoring responses to showcase how your skills align with their goals. By conveying your value with clarity and confidence, you establish a connection that sets you apart and leaves a positive impression.

Just remember, in order to communicate effectively the skill of listening is fundamental to enable you to have a balance of receive and transmit, in order for you to both understand and be understood.

Receive and Transmit

Most people do not listen with the intent to understand; they listen with the intent to reply."-Stephen R. Covey
Communication is more than the mere exchange of words it is the transfer of meaning, intent, and emotion. At its core, effective communication rests on three interdependent powers:

1. The Power to Understand – the ability to perceive the true meaning behind words, tone, and body language.
2. The Power to Receive – the capacity to be fully present and open, without judgment, while another speaks.
3. The Power to Transmit – the skill of expressing your thoughts clearly, authentically, and persuasively.

These three powers are not simply about speaking well or appearing articulate. They are deeply tied to active listening which is a skill that requires your complete intention, total humility, and focused presence. You will no longer fall into the trap of listening merely to respond, debate, or defend yourself. This "projection trap" can prevent from truly connecting, learning, and growing.

In this chapter we will explore listening, and how the ability to understand, receive, and transmit communication effectively is foundational to your Ultimate Success System for Life.

Understanding, Receiving, and Transmitting
Communication is like a three-step dance:
- Understanding is the mental and emotional alignment with the speaker's intent.
- Receiving is the openness to take in information without filtering it prematurely through personal biases.
- Transmitting is expressing a response or message that reflects clarity, empathy, and relevance.

When you master these steps, you create deep connection, emotional safety, and mutual growth.
As we examine listening further, you will see that active listening to others, to your own body, to feedback, and even to life itself becomes the catalyst for success in every domain.

Listening with your eyes;
The phrase "listen with your eyes" is psychologically profound. It suggests that true listening isn't just auditory, it's about receiving someone fully, with all your senses engaged.

What it means to listen with your eyes
- Non-verbal language is louder than words.
- Research shows that the majority of human communication is non-verbal, tone, gestures, posture, facial expressions.
- Eyes in this instance are used as antennas.
- Our eyes catch micro-expressions, shifts in energy, small hesitations, all of which reveal truths people may not voice.
- Listening with your eyes is silent listening.
- Sometimes, the deepest listening happens when no words are spoken, when your eyes show presence, and the other person feels seen.

Normally, "listening" is associated with ears and sound. But to truly listen:
- The ears catch words.
- The eyes catch feelings.
- The heart connects them.

So listening with your eyes means:
- Reading body language.
- Noticing when someone's smile doesn't match their tone.
- Seeing when silence is hiding pain or longing.
- Recognising that "I'm fine" spoken with a smile but empty eyes is not fine.

Psychological Depth

- Mirror neurons: Our brains mirror the emotions we see in others. Eye contact and subtle facial cues activate empathy pathways, letting us "feel" what the other person feels.
- Congruence: When words and eyes don't align, the eyes usually reveal the truth. (This is why people say: "Look me in the eye and say that.")
- Trauma & trust: For someone in pain, being "listened to with eyes" (eye contact, stillness, undivided attention) creates safety without them having to articulate everything.

In practice
To "listen with your eyes" is to:
- Give your undivided attention (no phone, no glancing around).
- Hold soft, steady eye contact (not staring, but open).
- Notice micro-signals: clenched jaw, fidgeting hands, eyes watering, posture shrinking.
- Respond with presence: sometimes a nod or softened gaze "says" more than words.

The greater theory
The ability to listen with your eyes suggests that listening is not just about sound at all, it's about presence.
- When we truly listen, we are absorbing the whole person, not just their voice.
- Eyes let us hear what's unsaid, what's hidden, what's fragile.
- It turns conversation into communion — a shared experience where someone feels completely seen.

Now let us see the effects of listening on the magnificent seven.

Sleep: Listening to Your Inner Signals

"When sleep is abundant, minds flourish. When it is deficient, they don't."- Matthew Walker (The Sleep Doctor)

Sleep is often sacrificed in the pursuit of productivity. Yet, listening to your body's signals is the first step toward reclaiming restorative rest.

Understanding Sleep Needs

Your body communicates exhaustion through yawns, difficulty focusing, irritability, and reduced physical performance. But in our busy lives, we often ignore these cues, convincing ourselves that more coffee or willpower will suffice.

For example, a high-achieving entrepreneur once bragged about working 20-hour days. Over time, his health declined, and his decision-making suffered. It wasn't until he listened to his body's fatigue signals and prioritised quality sleep that his performance and clarity improved.

Receiving Expert Advice

Many ignore sleep science, dismissing it as a luxury rather than a necessity. Yet research consistently shows that deep, consistent sleep improves memory, emotional regulation, and immune function. By receiving credible information, you align your habits with what your body truly needs.

Transmitting Clarity

Communicating your sleep needs to family, partners, or coworkers creates a supportive environment. For instance, setting boundaries like "I don't take calls after 9 PM" sends a message about your commitment to well-being.

Pitfall: Neglecting to listen inward leads to chronic fatigue, burnout, and diminished resilience.

Path of Mastery: Active listening fosters mental calmness, making sleep a powerful regenerative habit.

Health & Nutrition: Listening to Your Body and the Science

"The food you eat can be either the safest and most powerful form of medicine, or the slowest form of poison."
Ann Wigmore (Holistic health practitioner)

Health is not just about following trends; it's about understanding your unique needs, receiving trusted information, and transmitting those needs clearly to yourself and others.
Understanding Internal Signals
Your body constantly communicates through subtle signals—bloating, headaches, mood swings, energy dips—but most people ignore them. A friend who struggled with low energy realized after months of trial that her fatigue was tied to gluten intolerance. She finally learned to listen to her body's feedback after meals.

Receiving Wisdom
Health advice is abundant, but much of it is conflicting. Active listening means seeking qualified guidance—from doctors, nutritionists, and evidence-based sources—and not just following social media fads.

Transmitting Your Needs
If you are committed to healthy eating, you must communicate your needs when dining out or with family. Saying "I'm choosing whole foods to feel better" is a way of transmitting your commitment.

Pitfall: Dismissing signals and failing to listen to reliable guidance leads to preventable illness.
Path of Mastery: Active listening helps you make informed, conscious choices about what you consume, leading to vitality and longevity.

Exercise: Listening to Your Body in Motion

"Movement is a medicine for creating change in a person's physical, emotional, and mental states."- Carol Welch

Exercise is not just about doing more; it's about listening deeply to your body's capacity and limits.
Understanding Fatigue vs. Resistance
Many overtrain because they fail to differentiate between true exhaustion and mere mental resistance. Listening to your body helps you know when to push harder and when to rest. Professional athletes excel because they understand recovery is as important as effort.

Receiving Guidance
Trainers and coaches provide valuable feedback—but only if you're open to hearing it. Many people fail to improve because they reject constructive criticism or assume they know best.

Transmitting Goals
Sharing your fitness goals with a partner, coach, or workout community helps create accountability. For example, telling a trainer "I want to focus on strength rather than weight loss" ensures your program aligns with your intentions.

Pitfall: Ignoring feedback leads to injury or stagnation.
Path of Mastery: Active listening allows for smarter training, improved results, and sustainable fitness.

Education: Listening as a Gateway to Wisdom

"Wisdom begins in wonder."— Socrates

Education is one of the most direct domains where active listening transforms knowledge into wisdom.

Understanding Beyond the Words
In a lecture or conversation, there is always more than what is spoken. Great learners listen for nuance, tone, and the why behind the words. For instance, a law student who listened not just to the facts of a case but to the underlying reasoning excelled beyond peers who memorized mechanically.

Receiving Different Perspectives
True education requires humility to receive ideas that challenge your worldview. Listening actively to diverse perspectives—different cultures, disciplines, and experiences—broadens your understanding.

Transmitting Your Learning
When you teach or discuss what you've learned, you solidify understanding. Effective students listen deeply, then transmit knowledge through dialogue, teaching, or writing, reinforcing mastery.

Pitfall: Passive listening leads to surface-level learning.
Path of Mastery: Active listening turns education into a transformative journey, not just accumulation of information.

Relationships: The Art of Active Listening

"To listen is to lean in, softly, with a willingness to be changed by what we hear."— Mark Nepo

Perhaps no area suffers more from poor listening than relationships.

Understanding Emotional Layers
People often say one thing but feel another. A partner who says "I'm fine" may actually be hurt or anxious. Active listening—observing tone, body language, and context—reveals the truth beneath the surface.

Receiving Without Judgment
When you give someone space to express themselves without interruption or criticism, you create emotional safety. Couples who practice empathetic listening report greater intimacy and trust.

Transmitting With Clarity
Healthy relationships require clear, kind communication. For example, saying "I feel unheard when you interrupt me" transmits feelings without blame.

Example: In couples therapy, a man learned to stop planning his rebuttal while his wife spoke. When he finally listened just to understand, their marriage improved dramatically.

Pitfall: Listening only to respond breeds conflict and disconnection.
Path of Mastery: Deep listening strengthens empathy, trust, and love.

Financial Intelligence: Listening for Clarity and Opportunity

"Risk comes from not knowing what you're doing."— Warren Buffett

Financial success is built on listening to the right information, guidance, and trends.

Understanding the Language of Money
Many avoid financial education because they find it overwhelming. Active listening in financial seminars, mentorship, or investment discussions helps demystify complex concepts.

Receiving Mentorship
A young professional once doubled his savings by actively listening to a mentor explain compound interest and disciplined budgeting. Those who reject advice often remain trapped in cycles of poor money management.

Transmitting Confidence
Negotiating salaries, deals, or investments requires clear articulation. The more you listen and understand the other party's needs, the more effectively you can transmit your own value proposition.

Pitfall: Tuning out financial advice or failing to clarify leads to costly mistakes.
Path of Mastery: Active listening builds financial literacy, confidence, and resilience.

Work: Listening as a Leadership Superpower

"Leaders who don't listen will eventually be surrounded by people who have nothing to say." — Andy Stanley

In the workplace, listening is a key differentiator between mediocrity and excellence.

Understanding Team Dynamics
Great managers listen to team concerns, frustrations, and ideas. By understanding the unspoken needs of employees, they inspire loyalty and innovation.

Receiving Feedback
Professionals who accept constructive criticism grow faster. Those who dismiss feedback stagnate.

Transmitting Vision
A leader's ability to listen deeply allows them to craft and transmit a vision that resonates with their team. Steve Jobs was known for listening intently in design meetings before making decisive moves.

Pitfall: Talking more than listening creates disengagement and inefficiency.

Path of Mastery: Active listening fosters collaboration, creativity, and leadership excellence.

The Deeper Psychological Shift

Why do so many fail to listen?
- Ego: The need to be right overrides the desire to understand.
- Distraction: A busy, multitasking mind cannot be fully present.
- Fear: Silence and vulnerability make some uncomfortable, so they fill it with words.

Mastering listening requires humility (knowing you don't have all the answers), patience (allowing space for others), and presence (resisting internal and external distractions).
Integrating Listening into the Ultimate Success System
When you look at the Magnificent Seven, a pattern emerges:

- Sleep requires listening to your body's need for rest.
- Health and Nutrition require listening to internal signals and trusted guidance.
- Exercise requires listening to your body in motion.
- Education requires listening to learn and grow.
- Relationships require listening to build trust and intimacy.
- Financial Intelligence requires listening to wisdom and trends.
- Work requires listening to collaborate, lead, and innovate.

Active listening is the keystone habit that amplifies every other life mastery skill.

Conclusion
The power to understand, receive, and transmit is far more than a communication tool, it is a life mastery skill. It allows you to connect deeply, learn continuously, and lead effectively. Conversely, failing to listen leaves you trapped in misunderstandings, conflict, and stagnation.
When you learn to listen actively to others, to your own body, and to life itself you unlock clarity, connection, and contribution. You sleep better, eat better, move better, learn better, love better, earn better, and work better.

Chapter 12

The Path Forward

The Path Forward – Mastering the Magnificent Seven for Life

As we come to the end of this journey together, I want to leave you with a powerful truth: **mastery is not a destination, it is a continuous process of growth, refinement, and evolution.**

This book is not just about a set of habits to check off a list; it is a way of life, a framework that integrates seamlessly into every decision, action, and goal you pursue.
You now have the knowledge, the structure, and the power to take control of your life. But knowledge without action is meaningless. **The key to true transformation lies in consistently applying what you have learned, being disciplined in refining your habits, and striving for mastery in each of the seven foundational elements.**

The question you must now ask yourself is this: **What will I do with this knowledge?**
Will you let it fade into the background, another book on the shelf, another idea that sounded good in theory but never became a reality?
Or will you take full ownership of your future and commit to integrating these principles into the very fabric of your life?
The choice is yours.

The Interconnected Nature of the Magnificent Seven
The single most important message of this book is the **deep interconnectedness of these seven foundational habits.**
They do not exist in isolation. As we have discovered on this journey, each one of the habits affects and influences the others, creating a ripple effect that can either elevate or diminish your overall success and well-being.

- **Sleep** fuels your physical health, mental clarity, and emotional resilience, making it easier to make wise financial decisions, build strong relationships, and perform at your best in work and exercise.
- **Health and Nutrition** provide the raw materials your body and brain need to function optimally, supporting your ability to make sound judgments, sustain energy, and cultivate meaningful connections.
- **Exercise** strengthens your body and mind, boosting confidence, discipline, and vitality, all of which enhance your ability to manage finances, perform well in your work, and maintain fulfilling relationships.
- **Relationships** nourish your soul, providing support, accountability, and purpose that make every other endeavor more meaningful and rewarding.
- **Financial Intelligence** grants you the freedom to make choices that align with your values and aspirations, reducing stress and opening doors to greater opportunities.
- **Work** when pursued with passion and purpose, becomes a vehicle for contribution, growth, and fulfillment, elevating every other aspect of your life.

When you strengthen one area, the benefits naturally extend into the others. But the opposite is also true, neglecting one can create a cascade of negative consequences. This is why true mastery requires balance and commitment across all seven areas.

Mastery as a Lifelong Journey
One of the biggest traps people fall into is the belief that once they reach a certain milestone, whether it's financial success, a fit body, or a fulfilling relationship, they can stop growing. But the moment you stop growing, you start declining.

Mastery is not about perfection; it is about relentless progress. It is about committing to becoming a little better each day, refining your habits, and never settling for mediocrity. There will be setbacks. There will be moments of doubt, frustration, and even failure. But the difference between those who succeed and those who don't is **the ability to get back up, learn from mistakes, and keep moving forward.**

True mastery means **falling in love with the process of growth.** It means embracing challenges as opportunities to evolve. It means recognising that **every choice you make, no matter how small, either moves you closer to or further away from the life you desire.**

So, as you step forward with this book into the rest of your life, ask yourself:
- **How can I improve my sleep just 1% this week?**
- **What small change can I make in my diet to fuel my body and mind better?**
- **How can I challenge myself physically to grow stronger and more disciplined?**
- **What one thing can I do today to strengthen my relationships?**
- **What financial decision can I make today that will benefit my future self?**
- **How can I bring more passion, creativity, and purpose into my work?**

Small improvements, compounded over time, create extraordinary results.

The Responsibility to Share and Elevate Others
With great knowledge comes great responsibility. Now that you understand the power of the **Magnificent Seven**, you have an opportunity perhaps even a duty to share this wisdom with others.

The world is in desperate need of people who **live with purpose, lead by example, and inspire others to rise higher.** Imagine a society where more people prioritised their health, cultivated meaningful relationships, managed their finances wisely, and pursued work that truly mattered. Imagine how much suffering, stress, and unhappiness could be eliminated if more individuals embraced these principles.

This is about more than just **your** personal success **this is about elevating humanity itself.**

By living the **Magnificent Seven**, you become a beacon of possibility. Your transformation will naturally inspire those around you, your family, friends, colleagues, and even strangers. And when you share what you have learned, you create a ripple effect that extends far beyond what you can see.

This is how real change happens.
Not through grand, sweeping revolutions, but through individuals **who commit to personal excellence and inspire others to do the same.**

Will you take on this responsibility? Will you become not just a student of the **Magnificent Seven**, but a teacher, a leader, and a force for good in the world?

Your Next Steps

As you turn the final pages of this book, the real work begins. Here's how you can take immediate action to ensure that the **Magnificent Seven** becomes an unshakable foundation for your life:

1. **Review Your Current Habits** – Take an honest inventory of where you currently stand in each of the seven areas. What are your strengths? Where do you need the most improvement?
2. **Set Clear Goals** – Define specific, measurable goals for each of the **Magnificent Seven**. Whether it's improving your sleep, increasing your savings, deepening your relationships, or excelling in your work, write down what you want to achieve.
3. **Create an Action Plan** – Break your goals down into actionable steps. What can you do daily, weekly, and monthly to move closer to mastery in each area?
4. **Track Your Progress** – Regularly assess your growth. Keep a journal, use a tracking app, or create a habit scorecard to hold yourself accountable.
5. **Surround Yourself with Excellence** – Seek out mentors, join communities of like-minded individuals, and eliminate negative influences that hinder your progress.
6. **Teach What You Learn** – Share this knowledge with others. Teach your children, your friends, and your colleagues. Start conversations, lead by example, and be a force for positive change.
7. **Never Stop Learning** – Mastery is a lifelong journey. Continue to seek wisdom, challenge yourself, and refine your approach as you evolve.

The Future is Yours to Shape
The world is constantly changing, and with it, the challenges and opportunities you will face. But no matter what external circumstances arise, the principles of the **Magnificent Seven** will always remain relevant.

By integrating these habits into your life, you are not only securing your own success and fulfilment, you are contributing to a greater movement toward a more enlightened, empowered, and thriving humanity.

Imagine a world where more people are physically vibrant, mentally sharp, financially wise, and deeply connected to their purpose and each other. That world is possible. And it starts with **you.**

The **Magnificent Seven** is your foundation. But what you build upon it is entirely up to you.
So now, as you close this book, take a deep breath and make a decision.
Will you commit to **mastering the magnificent life that is within your reach?**

The Choice Is Yours!

Chapter 13

Philosophical Insights

Reclaim Your Direct Experience

To reclaim your direct experience means to return to life as it is actually happening right now, through your own senses rather than living through filters of distraction, habit, stress, or other people's opinions.

- Direct experience = what you see, hear, feel, taste, and sense in the present moment.
- Losing it = when we get caught up in stories, judgments, or living on autopilot, we no longer connect to what's real in front of us.
- Reclaiming it = choosing to be present again: tasting food fully, noticing the sound of a friend's voice, feeling your breath, walking without rushing.

It's a practice of shifting from thinking about your life, to actually experiencing your life.

In short: To reclaim your direct experience is to step out of your mind's chatter and step back into reality, as your body, senses, and heart are living it right now.

Your Daily Energy is a Precious Resource to be Invested Wisely

- Your daily physical, emotional, and mental energy should be channeled wisely.
- Every decision, task, or stressor impacts it, whether small or large.
- Recognising this keeps you intentional, making sure you focus your energy on what matters.
- The skill is learning to prioritise, recharge, and protect your energy so it fuels growth.

Solitude is Where You Get to Know Yourself
- In stillness and quiet, without external noise, you reconnect with your true self.
- Solitude strips away social masks and distractions, revealing your deeper thoughts, fears, and desires.
- It's not loneliness, it's conscious time with yourself.
- This is where reflection, healing, and authentic self-knowledge begin.

Trust Your Internal Guidance System
- Deep within, you have intuition, the "gut sense" or inner compass that often knows before logic does.
- In the rush of life, this voice rises with strength, outshining opinions, expectations, and fears.
- Solitude sharpens that inner signal, making it easier to hear and follow.
- Trusting it means honouring your values, instincts, and felt sense of what is right for you.

In essence:
Solitude is where you recharge, reflect, and reconnect. In that quiet space, you rediscover and trust your own inner compass, the guidance system that's been with you all along.

Simplicity vs Complexity: Simple Dedication to the Self to Live as Your Own Champion.

Simplicity vs. Complexity
- Life often feels tangled with obligations, noise, and endless choices. That's complexity.
- Simplicity is stripping back to what matters, the essentials that bring health, meaning, and peace.
- Complexity scatters your energy outward; simplicity focuses it inward and forward.
- The challenge is not adding more, but removing what dilutes your attention and drains your spirit.

Simple Dedication to the Self
- Dedication doesn't mean grand gestures, it means consistent, small acts of care.
- Resting when tired, nourishing your body, moving daily, protecting your mind from clutter.
- Simple dedication compounds: the little habits build resilience, confidence, and strength over time.

To Live Life as Your Own Champion
- A champion is someone who fights for, defends, and uplifts.
- To live as your own champion means not waiting for external validation, rescue, or permission.
- It's trusting yourself, backing yourself, and choosing actions that align with your values and well-being.
- Instead of self-criticism, you become your own advocate celebrating progress, learning from setbacks, and holding the vision of your best self.

In essence:
Simplicity over complexity means focusing on what truly matters to you. Dedication to the self means showing up daily for your own well-being. And being your own champion means carrying yourself with courage, loyalty, and belief, even when no one else is cheering.

Look at Your World With Fresh Eyes
- Fresh eyes = seeing things as if for the first time, without old assumptions, grudges, or autopilot thinking.
- Often, you don't see the world itself, you only see your stories about it.
- By choosing fresh eyes, you allow curiosity, openness, and possibility to enter.
- It's a practice of presence: asking "What's really here, now?" instead of recycling yesterday's lens.

Because the Way You View the World
- Your perception isn't neutral, it's shaped by your past experiences, beliefs, fears, and expectations.
- Two people can live the same day, yet one sees opportunity while the other sees only problems.
- The "view" you hold becomes a filter that colours every choice you make and every feeling you carry.

It's How You Choose to Live
- If you see the world as hostile, you live defensively.
- If you see the world as abundant, you live generously.
- If you see the world as fixed, you stay stuck.
- If you see the world as evolving, you grow.
- The quality of your life isn't determined just by events, but by the lens you choose to interpret them through.

In essence:
Looking at your world with fresh eyes means deliberately choosing a perspective of openness and renewal. Since perception shapes reality, the way you choose to see becomes the way you live.
This makes a powerful bridge into habit-building: if you want to live differently, you must first learn to look differently.

It is Better to Have Something and Not Need it, Than to Need it and Not Have it
- This points to the wisdom of preparation and foresight.
- Having tools, skills, or resources "just in case" gives you resilience and peace of mind.
- Examples: carrying water on a hike, learning basic first aid, saving money, or knowing how to cook healthy meals.
- Even if you never need them, their presence provides security.
- The pain of lack is far greater than the "burden" of preparedness.
- Being caught unready, without savings, without health, without knowledge, leads to crisis and regret.
- Needing and not having exposes fragility, while having and not needing reflects strength.

The Deeper Wisdom
- This principle isn't about hoarding or fear, it's about cultivating readiness.
- Applied to life, it means:
    - Build health now, so illness doesn't catch you unprepared.
    - Learn skills before you're desperate for them.
    - Save money before emergencies strike.
    - Strengthen relationships before you need support.
- It's living proactively instead of reactively.

In essence:
Preparation creates freedom. Having and not needing gives peace. Needing and not having creates suffering. The wise path is to quietly build reserves of strength, knowledge, and resilience before life demands them.

Keep Your Mind on Your Own Business

- Your attention is your greatest currency.
- Wherever your mind goes, your energy flows.
- If your thoughts are scattered across gossip, comparison, or judgment, you dilute your power.
- Mastery begins with focus: protecting your mental space and directing it where it matters.
- Literally: tend to your work, your goals, your finances, your growth.
- Figuratively: honor your own life path instead of trying to live through others.
- It means taking radical responsibility, not being distracted by what others are doing, achieving, or saying.
- In truth, "your business" is your health, your mindset, your purpose, your contribution.

The Deeper Wisdom
- Worrying about others' lives creates noise and envy.
- Focusing on your own cultivates peace, progress, and self-respect.
- It doesn't mean ignoring others, it means you stop leaking energy into things outside your control.
- Paradoxically, when you mind your own business, you end up being of more value to others, because you show up whole and steady.

In essence:
Keeping your mind on your own business is about protecting your mental energy, focusing on your growth, and living from self-responsibility rather than distraction or comparison. It's not selfishness, it's stewardship of your life.

Ask Yourself "What is my Why?"

- Growth starts with self-inquiry.
- Most people move on autopilot doing what's expected, following routines, chasing goals that aren't theirs.
- Pausing to ask yourself cuts through noise and reconnects you with your inner compass.
- It's not about what others think, it's about what truly drives you.
- Your why = your deeper reason, your source of fuel, the meaning behind your actions.
- It's the anchor that keeps you steady when motivation fades.
- A strong why transforms effort into purpose:
    - Work is no longer about "earning money," but about creating freedom or contribution.
    - Education is no longer about "getting it done," but about becoming the person you choose to be.

The Deeper Wisdom
- Without a why, success can feel empty.
- With a why, struggle feels more worthwhile.
- Your why evolves, what drives you at 20 may shift at 40. That's natural.
- The key is to keep asking, to keep realigning actions with meaning.

In essence:
Asking "What is my why?" is the practice of uncovering your true drive, the deeper reason behind your choices. It transforms discipline into devotion and keeps you walking through resistance because you're moving toward something that matters to you.

You are the Projector Not the Screen

- The projector generates the image. Likewise, your mind, beliefs, and inner state create the way you experience the world.
- Your thoughts, stories, and emotions color everything you perceive.
- If you carry anger, you project a hostile world. If you carry gratitude, you project abundance.
- You are the source, the origin of the picture you see.
- The screen is the external world, events, people, circumstances.
- Many believe life "out there" is causing their experience, but often it's the projection from within shaping how it looks.
- The screen only reflects what the projector beams onto it. Change the film inside, and the picture outside changes.
- You can't always control the screen, but you do control the projector.

The Deeper Wisdom
- Stop blaming the screen (the world, others, circumstances).
- Start adjusting the projector (your mindset, your choices, your inner story).
- This shift is empowerment: instead of reacting to what appears, you consciously create what you see.
- Life becomes less about "fixing the screen" and more about upgrading the projector.

In essence:
You are not a passive recipient of reality. You are the projector your inner world shapes your outer experience. The screen is only a reflection. Transform the projector, and the movie of your life transforms with it.

Nothing is as Good or as Bad as it Seems, it is the Thinking That Makes it so

- Your experiences themselves are neutral, events simply happen.
- What you label as "good" or "bad" is shaped by perspective, timing, and expectation.
- A setback today may later reveal itself as the very thing that sparked your growth.
- Likewise, a "good" fortune can bring challenges if not handled wisely.
- Life is rarely as extreme as your first impression of it.
- Your interpretation, the story you attach, creates the emotional weight.
- Two people can face the same situation and live completely different realities, depending on how they think about it.
- This means your suffering or joy isn't always in the event, but in the meaning you assign.

The Deeper Wisdom
- Freedom comes from seeing thought as thought, not absolute truth.
- If you can step back from the mind's story, the charge of "good" and "bad" softens.
- This allows you to meet life with equanimity: calmness and composure, especially in difficult situations. Less tossed around by extremes, more grounded in presence.
- It doesn't mean ignoring your feelings, it means recognising they arise from your interpretation, not only from reality.

In essence:
Events don't carry fixed labels of good or bad. It's your thinking that paints them that way. By understanding this, you gain power to shift perspective, reduce suffering, and meet your life with greater balance.

Take Responsibility of Your Energy

- Your energy isn't just physical, it's emotional, mental, and spiritual.
- Wherever you go, you bring an energetic imprint that influences people, situations, and even your own outcomes.
- Taking responsibility means owning the quality of that energy instead of unconsciously leaking stress, anger, or negativity onto yourself or others.
- Energy is both a personal resource and a collective ripple what you radiate shapes what you attract.
- Positive energy fuels growth: optimism, kindness, focus, vitality. It uplifts not only you but everyone around you.
- Negative energy drains: complaining, self-pity, resentment, neglect of the body. It spreads heaviness and blocks opportunities.
- Both are contagious, people feel your energy long before they process your words.

The Deeper Wisdom
- Energy is not neutral it's creative.
- By taking ownership, you stop blaming circumstances and start recognizing your role in shaping your experience.
- This doesn't mean forcing "positivity", it means cultivating awareness, shifting where possible, and learning from where you slip.
- You can't control every event, but you can choose the energy you bring to it.

In essence:
Your energy is your signature. Every thought, word, and action broadcasts either life-giving or life-draining force. Taking responsibility means consciously choosing how you show up because whether positive or negative, it always matters.

A Harmonious Resonance Creates a Stillness of the Mind

- Resonance means alignment, when different elements vibrate in sync with each other.
- In life, this can be your thoughts aligning with your values, your actions aligning with your intentions, or your inner world aligning with your outer world.
- Harmony is not perfection, but balance, a natural rhythm where nothing feels forced or out of place.
- When you are in harmony, your inner noise quiets.
- The constant push-and-pull of conflict, doubt, and contradiction dissolves.
- Stillness arises not by silencing your mind through force, but by removing your inner friction that makes it restless.
- This stillness is clarity: a calm space where your insight, creativity, and peace naturally emerge.

The Deeper Wisdom
- Your mind is noisy when it is fragmented, saying one thing, doing another, wanting one path but walking another.
- Bring your life into resonance (values, actions, energy), and your mind settles on its own.
- Harmony outside (with nature, music, relationships) can also create resonance within you, leading to calm presence.
- Stillness is not emptiness, it is a state of attunement, where you feel both grounded and alive.

In essence:
When your life vibrates in harmony with your values, your choices, your environment, your mind no longer needs to race or resist. Resonance naturally creates stillness, and in that stillness, you find peace and clarity.

Chapter 14

Life is a Skill

Life is a Skill

I'm 56 now, and if there's one thing I've learned, it's that life is a skill. You don't master it once and for all, you work at it, day after day, the same way you train your body. I still train hard every morning, not because anyone's watching, not because I need applause, but because the process itself matters to me.

The grind, the sweat, the small victories, that's where the joy is. Over the years I've come to see that thoughts, emotions, and actions are the real tools. Get your thoughts straight, control your emotions, and let your actions prove your intent. When those three line up, you feel solid. That's real freedom, not money, not status, but peace of mind. The silence that comes when you know you're living on your own terms.

Nobody gives you that freedom, you take it. You build it with patience, resilience, focus. I say it to myself all the time: focus, focus, focus. And before anything else work on yourself. If I'm not building myself, I'm building nothing.

So I keep going. I sharpen my tools, I embrace the process, and I create my own value. That is the work.
That is the freedom, and for me that is the living that may one day lead to wisdom.

Wisdom
The ultimate skill is knowing which tool to use when.
- Sometimes you need patience, sometimes urgency.
- Sometimes self-assertion, sometimes humility.
- Sometimes risk-taking, sometimes restraint.

Wise is the craftsman who can choose which tool serves the moment best.

Becoming Seasoned

People throw the word "seasoned" around like it's just another label, seasoned traveler, seasoned professional (or in my case, wrinkled old git). Truth is, you don't get seasoned just by getting old or clocking time. You get seasoned by living through the fire, by messing up, getting knocked down and standing back up, shaking it off and keeping at it when most people would have quit.

In my 56 years, I've earned a bit of seasoning. It didn't come easy. It came from busted plans and busted heads, long nights, heavy losses, and hard lessons. That's the seasoning, the scars that don't show on your skin (and the ones that do) but shape who you are. It's like food: throw raw meat on the grill and it's bland. Let it cook slow, let it soak up the spice, and it develops flavor. Life works the same way.

Being seasoned means you've taken the punches, and instead of folding, you learned how to move with them. It's resilience, it's grit, it's knowing when to push and when to let time do its work. For me, being seasoned isn't about slowing down. It's about carrying everything I've lived through into every round, every challenge, every day I get up and push myself beyond what I think I'm capable of.

That's seasoning. That's life, and if you learn to love it, there is no greater feeling than the flavour of experience from marinating in life itself. Just as a perfectly seasoned dish feels balanced, a seasoned person often embodies a kind of balance between confidence and humility, strength and softness, knowledge and curiosity.

The Power of Humour

If there's one thing that will carry you through life without breaking, it's a sense of humour. Not the shallow kind, forced jokes or pretending everything's fine. I'm talking about a deep, seasoned sense of humour. The kind that lets you grin at yourself when you make a total pigs tit of it. The kind that lets you shake your head and laugh when life deals you a bad hand and you thank the big fella for the challenge because you know there's a lesson to be learned.

I've lived long enough to see how easy it is to grow hard, bitter, or sour. People lose jobs, marriages, friends, health, they lose their edge, and then they lose their light. And when you lose your light, you stop living long before you stop breathing, as I know all too well. But humour is the spark that has always kept the fire alive.

See, humour doesn't erase pain. It doesn't fix what's broken. But it softens the blow. It gives you enough breathing room to keep moving. It's resilience wrapped in laughter. When you can laugh at your own mistakes, the world can't bury you.
And don't underestimate what humour does for connection. People are drawn to it. You don't have to be the loudest or sharpest in the room, but if you can find humour in life, people feel it. They trust it.

Now, let me be clear: humour isn't about dodging reality. It's not about hiding behind sarcasm or cracking jokes to avoid the truth. Humour is courage. It's standing in the middle of reality and saying, "Yeah, this is rough, but I'm still here, and I can still laugh despite the hefty kick in the teeth". That's strength. That's survival.

The ultimate success system for life isn't just discipline, hard work, or focus, it's about balance. And humor is balance. It keeps the weight of responsibility from crushing you. It gives you air in your lungs when pressure is tight around your chest.

At 56, I train every day (at a measured pace). I push my body which works ok when I'm warmed up but you don't want to watch me shuffling to the toilet at 3.00 in the morning bouncing off the doors and stubbing my toes. I sharpen my feeble mind, and I keep aiming higher even though I can't even see the target now, I know it's there.

But just as important, I laugh. I laugh at myself when I stumble which is all the time. I laugh at how serious I used to be and catch myself when I still am. I laugh at the absurdity of chasing perfection when life's always going to be messy. That laughter it's freedom.

So here's the truth: without a sense of humour, life is heavier than it has to be. With it, even the toughest load can be carried. Humour doesn't just help you survive, it keeps you seasoned, keeps you human, keeps you light on your feet even when the years stack up.

Because if you can still laugh, you can still live. And that, my friend, is its own success.

A Final Message

From the bottom of my heart thank you for making space in your life to take the time to read this book.

I would love the book to be a working document that helps you understand yourself in the moment, whatever your stage in life. I was also hoping to get the message across that sometimes in life there are dark times, and times when you think you're doing everything right and it feels like it's still not working. In those periods though, you can now look to see if your magnificent seven are in sync.

No panic, if one or more are a bit off and require adjustment in order to course correct then you know exactly what you need to do so you can continue to resonate on your highest frequency. Be bold and take action without apology.

My only ask is that if you see someone struggling or a bit lost in life and you think the information in these pages may help them in some small way then please do not hesitate to share it.

It may be just what they need to understand that the magic inside them still exists, and by living the ultimate success system for life, you can show them how they too can bring their magic into the life of others.

You began this journey by answering a simple but powerful question: **What Are The Top Ten Things You Currently Value Most In Your Life?**
Along the way, you've walked through lessons, stories, and tools, all designed to help you rethink your list, sharpen your focus and strengthen your resolve while carving out the life you chose.
Now, as you stand at the end of these pages, I leave you with a reminder, your list not of theory, but of practice.

1. Sleep.
2. Health and nutrition.
3. Exercise.
4. Education.
5. Relationships.
6. Financial intelligence.
7. Work.
8. Discipline.
9. Integrity.
10. Consistency.

These are not just words on a page; they are the foundations of your ultimate success system for life. They are the non-negotiable pillars that support freedom, peace of mind, and fulfilment.

Whenever life feels heavy, whenever the path ahead seems uncertain, come back to this list. Let it ground you. Let it remind you of what truly matters.
Because success is not a single moment, it is the daily process of honouring these values and living them fully, one choice at a time.

Carry this with you and continuously build on your system.
And remember, you hold the tools to the life you choose in the palm of your hand.

The Ultimate Success System For Life.

Acknowledgements

I have reached the end of this book, but the truth is the journey is not over just yet. Nobody gets anywhere alone. We are all carried, challenged, and sharpened by others along the way, and I'd be lying if I didn't pause here to acknowledge that.

First, to the people who believed in me, even when I didn't believe in myself, thank you, your quiet words of encouragement, your faith, and sometimes just your presence gave me the strength to keep moving forward with this project, and I shall continue to draw from it as the future unfolds.

To my family, friends, training partners, and every stranger who ever offered a kind word or a hard truth, of which there was plenty, you have all seasoned me. You've been part of the process, part of the fire that still burns deep inside me, part of the laughter that keeps me alive.

And finally, to the roller coaster ride of life itself, I thank and give gratitude for the storms and the knock downs, for the grind, for the bruises and the countless blessings. You have and will always be my greatest teacher.

This book may carry my name, but it also carries the fingerprints of everyone and everything that has shaped me. For that, I am deeply grateful and feel truly blessed.

What's next

I am currently working on developing an Inspired Nation Podcast where the goal is to reach and inspire as many people to become the best version of themselves by watching and listening to other inspirational people who have great stories to tell, both new and old, and hopefully see the magic that lies in everyone of us shed its full light on the world.
Together we can create a growing community to spread a whole load of inspiration across the nation and beyond.

I'm also working on The BOGA Philosophy which stands for Beast Often Gentleman Always and is linked to my background and my love of boxing, and will act as an accompaniment to the ultimate success system for life and is about cultivating and controlling ones inner beast whilst also embracing a life of the consummate gentleman.

Like this book it's about balancing different elements of ones inner and the outer worlds.

Printed in Dunstable, United Kingdom